THE COCKNEY (

Authentic cockney recipes – spiced with insights
into the lives of London's real East Enders

Brian Murphy
with additional material by Jack Hamm

Illustrations by Dawn Bradshaw

One of The London Pride
Collection
Comerford & Miller

The Cockney Cookbook was first published in 1989.
Reprinted 1991, 1995 by Comerford & Miller.

Second enlarged edition published in 1998 by
Comerford & Miller, 36 Grosvenor Road, West Wickham, Kent, BR4 9PY

UK Distributors: Central Books, 99 Wallis Road, London, E11 5LN

Cover design: Ad Lib Design, London, N19 / (0171) 263-1531

Printed and bound in Malaysia.

A Catalogue record for this book is available from the British Library.

ISBN 1 871204 10 0

BRIAN MURPHY, historian and food and drink expert, was the author of nine books. They include the definitive *World of Whisky*. He was a former director of the *Good Food Guide* and wrote many hundreds of articles for national newspapers and magazines.

His career included seaman, planter, librarian, and polytechnic lecturer. He was Britain's first Head of Television for the EEC.

His deep interest in London's eating habits and the practical need to find dishes to interest his children inevitably led him to explore the exciting world of cockney cooking. He died in 1996.

Acknowledgements First Edition
My thanks are due to Paul Corrigan of Corrigan Brothers, Jim Eva, manager of Corrigan Brothers, Tufnell Park Branch, the London Museum of Jewish Life, the Guildhall Museum, my publishers Terry Comerford and Russell Miller for practical suggestions and recipes, further recipes from Jean Brown and Marlene Crilly and to my aunt Irene Murphy for deciphering my appalling handwriting.
Brian Murphy 1988

Acknowledgements Second Edition
The names of many people who have contributed to the second edition are unknown. Several recipes were given in a radio phone-in with Brian Murphy and their names were never recorded. Other ideas, such as the inclusion of items on the Kray Brothers, Jack the Ripper, and the Match Girls were made to me in a somewhat inebriated conversation I had in an East End hostelry! However, I acknowledge the help given to me by Dr Edith Holding, Terry Miller, Erica Vincent, and Joan Moss. The publishers have asked me to record their thanks for the work of Jeanette Searles in preparation of this new edition.
Jack Hamm 1998

Introduction to Second Edition

Since its publication in 1998 the *Cockney Cookbook* has never been out of print. Copies have found their way to the USA where there are many families who can trace their roots to London's East End. More difficult to explain are orders from as far away as Japan!

There are no Cockneys in Tokyo but their influence spreads. Many Londoners, born far from London's East End, still call themselves – and are called – Cockneys. Rhyming slang, like *Dog and Bone* for *Phone,* the lively language of the Cockneys is widely used – even in TV commercials.

When this book was launched both the author and the publishers assumed that the Cockneys were a dying breed. This was before the popular BBC programme *EastEnders* took off. East London readers have reminded us that the land of the Cockneys still has a vibrant culture of its own.

Perhaps the secret of the book's success is the publication of unpretentious recipes linked to their social background. The Cockneys had to use what was to hand. For most of the time they wanted uncomplicated dishes which were easy to prepare. Today is not very different: families open the fridge and use what is available and they want cooking which is quick and easy. There are no recipes in the *Cockney Cookbook* which demand freshly picked golden thyme or arborio rice.

By all means add and substitute the ingredients in these basic recipes. That is how they have been used for generations. For this reason the publishers have ignored advice and kept to the format of the first edition. Ingredients are not listed separately but kept within the body of the text. Weights are given in Imperial measure but metric conversions are given at the back of the book. Except where stated, all meals are for four adults.

The publishers have however, taken most readers' suggestions on board. There are more historic notes on the East End, especially those events whose sites have become tourist attractions. The additional recipes are from genuine East London sources.

Brian Murphy died in 1996. He had no part in preparing the second edition but we trust readers will agree that the editors have captured his whimsical style in this publication.

Jack Hamm
September 1998

CONTENTS

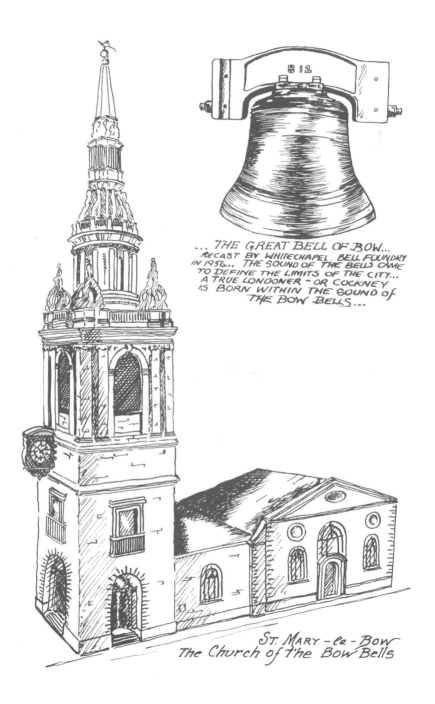

... THE GREAT BELL OF BOW ...
RECAST BY WHITECHAPEL BELL FOUNDRY
IN 1956 ... THE SOUND OF THE BELLS CAME
TO DEFINE THE LIMITS OF THE CITY ...
A TRUE LONDONER - OR COCKNEY
IS BORN WITHIN THE SOUND OF
THE BOW BELLS ...

ST. MARY - le - BOW
The Church of the Bow Bells

Who were the Cockneys?

True Cockneys came from a very small part of London when London was the world's biggest and most populous city. Traditionally, only those born within the sound of Bow Bells, which rang out from St Mary-le-Bow church Cheapside, could call themselves Cockneys.

But the true cockney heartland lay further east and is now almost entirely submerged in the new London Borough of Tower Hamlets. This was the poorest part of London and the homes they lived in, the clothes they wore and the jobs they did reflected this. Cockneys were poor. Many lived on the precarious borderline between malnutrition and starvation. To survive they had to be streetwise, sharp and quick thinking. Many of them spent most of their lives legally sailing very close to the wind. Their common and all-embracing poverty made them intensely loyal to each other and equally suspicious and contemptuous of outsiders. To cement loyalty they even invented a private language of their own, 'rhyming slang'.

Chronic and generational malnutrition meant that most Cockneys were physically small. But with this smallness came a liveliness and perkiness which found its perfect embodiment in their most familiar bird – the cheeky, bold and ubiquitous cock sparrow. Hence their most familiar form of endearment – "my old cock-sparrer". They were proud to be who they were – an exclusive and special breed of Londoner.

The food they ate had to be cheap, tasty and nourishing. They liked salty and spicy food – saveloys, faggots and kippers and bloaters. They liked gelatinous meats and dishes – cowheel, pigs' trotters, tripe and – a great favourite – jellied eels. And they liked sharp and vinegary sauces to go with them.

They liked strong cheeses too – Gorgonzola, Double Gloucester, Cheddar, strong pickles and relishes – pickled onions, Worcester sauce and brown sauce. Above all they liked cheap seafood – whelks, cockles and mussels, winkles and shrimps. Stalls selling these delicacies can still be found outside East End pubs – and not only East End pubs.

Their drinks had to be strong and full flavoured too – "tea you can stand your spoon up in", treacly stout and mild ale, bitingly dry London gin. They needed food and drink to "give a bit of relish" to a life that all too often was hard and cruel.

Many of their favourite dishes survive today. Many only exist in small and specialised outlets. This book is an attempt to introduce them to a wider world and in doing so to recreate just some of the atmosphere that was the breath of life to London's ancient and unique breed of Cockney.

Pickles and Relishes

In most London fish and chip shops you will still see big jars of pickles, onions, eggs and cucumbers. The latter in fact, are not so much relics of cockney London as Jewish London, dating from the mass immigration of Russian and Polish Jews in the earliest years of the century.

Cockney mums would have made their own pickled onions – and pickled cabbage and piccalilli too – since the basic ingredients were very cheap.

Cockney Pubs

Sadly, the last few years have seen the insides ripped out of many old cockney pubs to satisfy the new trend towards family meeting places with soft music, carpet and modern furniture. But Victorian brewers had a different market in mind and they spared no expense in their (successful) attempts to part the cockney from his pay packet. They lavished rich mahogany, expensive etched glass and plentiful brass on their pubs and there are luckily still a few of them left to the diligent searcher in Bethnal Green, Bow and other parts of the East End. In some you can buy pickled eggs still made to the recipe given.

Etiquette was rigid. There was the saloon bar for the cockney aristocracy, bookmakers, stallholders and successful pickpockets and those who had money to burn. The beer was more expensive here and gin and brandy popular. Then there was the 'spit and sawdust' public or four-ale bar where the beer was cheap and the fittings cheap with it.

For the ladies who were not allowed into the other bar, with the exception of 'those kind of women', there was the parlour with its plush chairs and benches where they could partake of their stout, their port and lemon or their gin and water. Finally there was the jug and bottle where people – often children – would come with their jugs, bottles and even saucepans to take away beer to be consumed off the premises.

The whole social edifice was controlled by the publican, a hateful figure to many impoverished cockney housewives. He would operate a strict, 'no credit' regime and decide whom he would allow into his palatial establishment. Many such pubs had a 'No Soldiers Here' poster in their windows. Soldiers were known to be heavy drinkers but also liable to break the place up when they had 'one over the eight'.

Pickled Onions

This is good with cheese and cold meats.

There are literally hundreds of recipes for making pickled onions
– and all of them are right. Peel small onions, cover them with
vinegar – that is the basic recipe. From here on, the variations
are indefinite. Here is my favourite:

Peel small onions and steep them in strong brine, three pounds
of salt to a gallon of water for two days. This drains out some of
the moisture in the onions.

If you want to use spiced vinegar, boil a handful of
peppercorns, a root of ginger, some mustard seeds, a chilli and a
stick of cinnamon in a quart of vinegar and let cool. Fill a jar
with the drained and dried onions, forcing them in to cram the
jar. Pour over the vinegar to cover the onions. Leave them a
month – eat within the year.

For alternative recipes, use clear distilled vinegar, try boiling
the onions for a few minutes, or use shallots instead of onions.
They are all fine by me. It is worth experimenting. Each cockney
household had its own favourite recipe. Try and find one your
family prefers.

Piccalilli

Piccalilli satisfied the Cockney's taste for strong flavours and
the need to be thrifty. You can use a mixture of almost any
low priced vegetables, onions, cauliflower, marrows, green
beans, red or green tomatoes and even cooking apples.
Providing the bad pieces are cut out, damaged vegetables can
be used.

Discard the leaves and stalks from the cauliflower and cut
into small florets. Dice the rest of the vegetables and soak all
the vegetables, fully submerged, in a brine solution (five
ounces to a gallon of water) for a day. Drain off and wash in
cold water.

To make mustard sauce, for each two pounds of vegetables
you will need three ounces of sugar, half an ounce of dry
mustard, one level teaspoon ground ginger, one pint of
vinegar, one ounce of cornflower and one level tablespoon of
turmeric.

Mix the sugar, mustard and ginger with three-quarters of a
pint of vinegar in a large saucepan, bring to the boil and add
the vegetables. Bring to the boil again, cover and simmer for
fifteen minutes. Blend the turmeric and cornflower in the
remaining vinegar and add to the pan. Boil for a further two
minutes. Pack the vegetables into jars, top up with the
remaining sauce and seal immediately. Ready for use in three
weeks.

Green Tomato Chutney

The cockney climate meant that his tomatoes, whether from allotment or window box, seldom all ripened and the cockney gardener would be left with several pounds of green and unripe fruit. His wife would seize these avidly, chop them roughly, add spiced vinegar (*see Pickled Onions*), sugar, sultanas, sliced onions and any other handy fruit. The quantities can be very much to your own particular taste. The vinegar should just cover the chopped tomatoes. The sugar should be at least half a pound to a pint of vinegar, or more if the tomatoes are very hard and green. Boil the mixture. The chutney is cooked as soon as the green fruit softens. Keep this pickle for a week or two before use.

Not only excellent with cold meats but can make all the difference when added to a beef or mutton casserole.

Pickled Red Cabbage

Goes well with cheese, cold meat, fish, baked potatoes and salads.

Take a firm red cabbage and slice it, the hard white centre included. Sprinkle salt over it, turning it so that the salt coats all the strips. Turn it twice a day for three days, adding a little more salt each time. It will now become limp and exude a dark red liquid – but don't worry! It will crisp beautifully in the pickle. Drain and dry it and fill it into jars. Cover with vinegar, spiced if you prefer. (*See recipe for pickled onions*).

Leave for two weeks, by which time it will be bright red, crisp and delicious.

Marrow Pickle

Take a large marrow, peel it, cut it in half and take out the seeds, and all the spongy flesh surrounding them. Cut the halved marrow into small squares, about one inch across. Add a pound of peeled pickling onions. Lay both of these on a flat dish, sprinkling on plenty of salt so that all the marrow pieces and onions are well salted. Leave for a day then you will find that a lot of water has drained off. Pour this away and put the marrow-onion mixture into a large saucepan with an ounce of ground ginger, an ounce of turmeric, a couple of chillies, half a pound of sugar and six pints of vinegar. Boil up and simmer until the mixture thickens. Allow to cool and put into jars.

elicious with cold
neat sandwiches or
s a snack by
nemselves.

Pickled Eggs

A very simple recipe. Hardboil eggs, peel them and cover with vinegar. This is all!

But here are a few tips that are useful. Use clear distilled vinegar because brown vinegar makes the eggs look muddy rather than an appetising white. Leave for at least a month. Decorate the pickle with a couple of bright red chillies or strips of brightly coloured pepper – this adds a little zest to the pickle too.

The Cockney Publican the 'Guv'ner'

A Modern Touch

Today's East Enders have embraced modern technology, a microwave oven will feature in most kitchens. Though we know their grand parents liked a good fry up, this is inadvisable on a micro but the same ingredients can be grilled. Just as tasty but with less cholesterol.

Modern Cockneys still need meals that take little time to cook. Leading busy lives they see no reason why cooking should be a time-consuming chore. Quick and easy is their motto.

The microwave recipes given are all traditional cockney fare. If you want to stick to conventional cooking, look in the index for cooking instructions.

The EastEnders

In February 1985, the BBC launched a new soap centred on London's East End, called appropriately *EastEnders*. It has been a remarkable success, by 1997 claiming peak viewing of nearly 10m. How accurately does it reflect the real East End, home of the Cockneys?

Albert Square, with its Queen Victoria pub would be familiar to the Cockneys of a century ago, as would the social life centred around the Pub. Mixed ethnic groups – most of them speaking with cockney accents – have been a familiar sight in the East End for at least one hundred and fifty years. Long before Asian and Caribbean families made the East End their home, the Irish and then the Jews became immigrant cockneys.

Most East Enders are still poor, many pinning their hopes of escape on finding profitable self employment that can be expanded into a successful business. These aspects of the East End are accurately recaptured in the BBC soap. The cockney accent is preserved. At onetime all the actors playing 'local' characters had to assure the BBC that they were East Enders born and bred.

While popular papers still describe the characters as Cockneys, the word is never used in the script. The accents may be authentic but the dialogue never captures the colourful language of the East End. There is no rhyming slang and no one has described a mean trick as 'a diabolical liberty'. But then, as the BBC would say, *EastEnders* is entertainment not anthropology.

Shepherd's Pie

You can prepare the mashed potato topping by microwave but it saves no time. Mash your potatoes the conventional way, while you use your micro to prepare the pie.

Set your oven to high. Spread a chopped onion over the base of a large casserole, cover with cling film, puncture the top and cook for 4 minutes. Add 1½ lb of minced beef to the onions, season, cover and cook for 15 minutes stirring every three minutes.

Spread the potatoes over the meat and cook uncovered for 4 minutes. If you want a nice crispy top you will have to brown under the traditional grill.

Quick Curry

Put a tablespoon of oil in a casserole dish with one large chopped onion. Add about six oz of diced vegetables like peppers, carrots or partly cooked potatoes. Add salt and two teaspoons of curry powder. Cover with cling film and puncture. Cook on High for 3 minutes.

Toss ½ lb of minced meat in about 2 tablespoons of flour and put this in the casserole. Cover with a plate not the casserole cover, as we want a loose fit. Cook on High for 10 minutes. Then stir again, re-cover and cook on Medium for 10 minutes.

Add a tin of chopped tomatoes, ½ pint of beef stock. Stir, re-cover and cook on medium for 10 minutes. If it is not thick enough, add a liquid paste of a little flour and water, stir in. Cover and cook on medium for 2 minutes. To let the curry blend, stand for a few minutes. If it gets too cold, reheat for a further 2 minutes; don't forget to give it a stir.

Sweet Piccalilli

This is an amazingly simple way to make this popular preserve. Prepare 2 lb of vegetables in the same way as given in the last section 'Pickles' but make sure there are onions in the mix.

Blend 3 oz of sugar with two teaspoons of dried mustard and a level teaspoon of ginger with ½ pint of the vinegar in a large bowl. Add the vegetables and mix well. Cover with cling film, puncture top and cook on high for 15 minutes.

Blend 2 tablespoons of flour with a teaspoon of turmeric and a ¼ pint of vinegar, stir into the mixture. Cook uncovered, on high for a further 5 minutes.

Put the vegetables into warmed sterilised jars and top up with the remaining sauce.

Fish

Although the great Billingsgate fish market was not far from where they lived, Cockneys were very conservative about fish. They knew what they liked – and that wasn't very much. For instance, tinned salmon was a rare and much appreciated treat – fresh salmon they never saw. Even fish as cheap and plentiful as fresh herrings or mackerel never played a major part in the Cockney's diet. He liked his fish salty and smoky – accompanied by lots of strong tea and thick slices of bread and butter. This old tradition still lives on in some East End fish and chip shops. Unless you specify to the contrary, they will serve your skate and chips with a plate of thick bread and butter and a mug of strong tea.

Billingsgate

The new Billingsgate fish market opened its doors on the Isle of Dogs in January 1982. Gone are the porters' age-old leather helmets, popularly supposed to have been modelled on those worn by Henry V's bowmen at Agincourt. Gone too are the teetering piles of baskets which the porters so nonchalantly carried on them. In their place are forklift trucks and computerised storage areas. The traditionally colourful language remains exactly the same!

The original market near the Tower of London was in existence as early as 1016, when the market sold fruit, corn and salt as well as fish. Six hundred years later it had become 'a free and open market for all sorts of fish' and has continued so until today.

Cockney costermongers and street traders would have come to Billingsgate to buy their wares – fresh herrings, cockles and mussels, shrimps, flounders, whelks and eels and all the other fishy delicacies so much enjoyed by their cockney customers. Most of them would have been more than competent in exchanging 'compliments' with the fish salesmen there!

Bloaters

Bloaters – the original 'red herrings' – are fresh herrings,
gutted but not split, and lightly salted and smoked. The best
way to cook bloaters is to slash lightly the sides of the fish and
grill under a hot grill until the skin begins to blister. Serve with
tea and bread and butter – but not so strong and thick as those
which go best with the noble kipper.

Bloaters are a delicately smoked fish and are now quite rare.
They have not been seen in Cockney-land for many years,
although they can still be found in Yarmouth and thereabouts.
But Cockneys loved them as a dish for 'high tea', a substantial
early evening meal.

Sprats

Sprats are little fish of the herring family; they are not young
herrings. They are caught in great quantities off the east coast of
England and come very fresh to the cockney market stalls. The
squeamish would cut the heads off and try to gut them, but this is
an operation analogous to milking a mouse. Forget it!

For the Cockney – and for me – there is only one way of
cooking sprats. Put a knob of butter or some cooking oil in a
frying pan and heat it until it is smoking hot. Meanwhile toss the
sprats in some seasoned flour. Throw the sprats into the hot oil
by the handful until they are crisp and brown, shaking the pan so
that they are crisped all over. Serve them hissing hot with bread
and butter and tea. Because you cannot possibly cook a meal of
sprats in one go, the cook has to devise his or her own method of
sharing the batches of sprats among the hungry guests.

Kippers

Most kippers you buy today alas, are half smoked and then
dipped in a flavoured dye. But your real kipper is a big fresh
herring, gutted and split and slowly smoked over oak sawdust.
Such a kipper, grilled, is a feast for a king.

There are a number of ways of cooking kippers. For delicate
stomachs who find the oily saltiness of the fish too strong, put
the kipper tail-up in a jug of boiling water for four minutes and
serve with a knob of butter.

The Cockney and the connoisseur prefer their kipper as God
intended – grilled. Get the grill very hot. Grill the kipper skin
side down for a minute or until the skin begins to shrivel. Turn
over and grill until the fish begins to smoke. Serve with bread
and butter and strong tea.

The bread and butter and strong tea are not only the perfect
accompaniment to a grilled kipper but are highly therapeutic if
a kipper bone gets caught in your throat.

Shared Tastes

Both the very rich and the very poor
have one thing in common; they are not
fussy about where their food has come
from. It is only the middle classes who
turn their noses up at the stranger
contents of the pig or the funny bits of
fish. The connoisseurs of Curzon Street
and Clapton both tucked into such
delicacies with relish.

They found that the more
unmentionable parts of flesh, fowl and
fish were often the tastiest if they were
properly prepared. So both the Chef in
London's most exclusive club and
restaurant and the humble cockney
mother in the East End would prepare
the same dishes. Only the names would
be different.

Costermongers

In Shakespeare's time, the costermonger, already a familiar figure, sold apples,
or 'costards'. But by the time of Queen Victoria, costermongers sold fruit,
vegetables, fish and all kinds of produce from their barrows. One historian
describes them: "They were a rough, quarrelsome, illiterate and virile set of men,
much given to fighting, drinking, and gambling, to tattooing their arms and
throwing bricks at policemen. Few of them could read or write, few troubled to
marry the woman they lived with, most – though not above cheating their
customers – were honest amongst themselves; and kind to their children and
donkeys".

Costermongering was the most typical of all cockney trades. If you were a
costermonger, you were a Cockney. You liked flash clothes, beer and gambling –
but especially beer. At one time four hundred public houses depended almost
entirely on costermongers for their trade. Their descendants still operate in
London's many markets, just as persuasively and noisily. You can find these
street markets all over London, many of them specialising in vegetables, clothes
or pets. Their trading practices have altered with the growth of the supermarkets;
they must offer competitive prices to survive and many will even exchange faulty
goods. The most famous London cockney market is Petticoat Lane, but you will
never find this on a street map: its official title is 'Middlesex Street'.

Fish Pie

This was a way of using up scraps of fish which could be bought cheaply at the fishmonger. Avoid very oily or bony fishes like herrings, which are better prepared in other ways anyway. It is basically a shepherds pie, but using fish, rather than meat.

Simmer the fish pieces in water with a few peppercorns and a sprig or two of parsley, until the fish is tender and the bones come out easily. Remove all the bones – all the bones.

Boil and mash potatoes. Take half of this mash, mix with the fish, half and half. Put this mixture in a pie dish and cover, with the rest of the mashed potato. You can, if you like, grate some cheese over the top for an extra tasty dish. Brown in a hot oven.

Smoked Haddock in Milk

I have never met anyone who didn't like this dish, being both very tasty, very nourishing but not very fattening. Put the piece or pieces of haddock in a saucepan, just cover with milk, add a knob of butter and a generous shake of white pepper and cook for ten minutes or until you can easily pierce the fish with a fork. Do not add salt as the fish is already salted. Serve with bread and butter and strong tea.

Roe on Toast

There is no agreement as to the relative merits of hard or soft herring roes but I must admit to being a soft man myself. All you need to do is to flour and fry roes in a little butter and serve them on hot buttered toast, lightly peppered and salted.

For a richer dish poach the roe for 10 minutes in water with a little salt and vinegar. Dice the roe and put into melted butter sauce with a little cream, then serve on toast as before. I must confess the last suggestion is not a traditional cockney recipe, it is a modern refinement offered to me by East End friends.

The Deserving Poor

In 1865 a Methodist Minister, William Booth, set up a mission to evangelise and to feed London's poor. It was the foundation of the Salvation Army. The desperately poor would be offered a bowl of hot soup and a hunk of bread. Soup kitchens were not unique to London's East End they were – and alas still are – found world-wide.

Soup offers a very sustaining meal and nothing is wasted. Boiling extracts nutriment from often inedible items like gristle and bones. Almost any thing can go into a soup – even some fruits.

The organisers of a fund raising cheese and wine party, who ladle out soup as an extra will use whatever is to hand. Perhaps bulking it up with pasta or noodles, instead of bread. But the principle is the same – an upmarket soup kitchen.

Cook Books

Traditional Cockney recipes were handed down from mother to daughter. The old Cockney mum would have felt no need for cook books. Mrs. Beaton's *Book of Household Management* would have seemed quite irrelevant with its advice on how to deal with domestic servants.

Perhaps the exception was Mr. Charles Elme Francatelli's *A Plain Cookery Book for the Working Classes,* first published in 1850. His focus was on an odd choice of readership for a man who had been Maitre D'Hotel and Chief Cook to Queen Victoria but no doubt he shared the sentiments of his times. Sympathy for the *deserving* poor and encouragement for the doctrine of self help.

Some Cockney women may have complained that the Queen's Cook had just copied their own recipes, even if this was so, he gave sound advice on preparation and flavoring. He advocated steaming vegetables rather than boiling. Many East End clergy found his book useful in advising their less provident parishioners.

Those with the care of the poor would have referred to his book in which he published three recipes on how to prepare a large quantity of good soup for the poor and four on the preparation of healthy gruel.

How to Prepare a Large Quantity of Good Soup for the Poor

It is customary with most large families, while living in the country, to kill at least some portion of the meat consumed their households; and without supposing for a moment that any portion of this is ever wasted.

I may be allowed to suggest that certain parts, such as sheep's heads, plucks, shanks, and scrag-ends, might very well be spared towards making a good mess of soup for the poor.

The bones left from cooked joints, first baked in a brisk oven for a quarter of an hour, and afterwards boiled in a large copper of water for six hours, would readily prepare a gelatinised foundation broth for the soup; the bones, when sufficiently boiled, to be taken out. And thus, supposing that your copper is already part filled with the broth made from bones (all the grease having been removed from the surface), add any meat you may have, cut up in pieces of about four ounces of weight, garnish plentifully with carrots, celery, onions, some thyme, and ground allspice, well-soaked split peas, barley, or rice; and, as the soup boils up, skim it well occasionally, season moderately with salt, and after about four hours' gentle and continuous boiling, the soup will be ready for distribution.

It was the custom in families where I have lived, as cook, to allow a pint of this soup, served out with the pieces of meat in it, to as many as the recipients' families numbered; and the soup was made for distribution twice every week during winter.'

These recipes are taken verbatim from 'Plain Cookbook for the Working Classes'.

Cod's Head

"First make some stuffing with one pound of bruised crumbs of bread mixed with six ounces of chopped suet, two eggs, chopped parsley, onions and thyme. Put this stuffing inside the cod's head, and place it in a baking dish with two ounces of butter, a pint of vinegar, and a pint and a half of water. Spread a little butter all over the cod's head, and then a thick coating of breadcrumbs all over it, bake it for an hour in the oven. A few oysters would be an improvement".

Sounds pretty good to me! The inclusion of oysters might confuse the reader who is told the Cockneys were poor. Don't forget that oysters were very cheap at that time.

Bangers

Sausages, known throughout London as 'bangers', were for many Cockneys the basis of a quickly prepared meal. Today we are familiar with the richly spiced continental sausage and very good they are, but the flavours of our more traditional bangers should not be overlooked.

King of them is still the saveloy. A common sight once in eel and pie shops, fish and chip shops and many pubs, was a big, brightly polished copper container. This was a saveloy heater. In it, saveloys were kept hot and moist over a water bath.

Rhyming Slang

Like many other close communities, the cockneys had a large number of words and catch-phrases which had special meanings for them. "Give us a bash at the bangers and mash" of the popular song is an example. But they took this to extremes by inventing a whole new language – rhyming slang. It worked by using a phrase that rhymed with a word rather than the word itself and then shortening the phrase to its non-rhyming part. Thus 'stairs' became 'apples and pears' and then simply 'apples'. 'Hat' became 'Tit for tat' and then simply 'titfer'.

'Lies' became 'pork pies', hence 'telling porkies' for not telling the truth. The origin of the slang 'to grass', describing the betrayal by criminals of their colleagues to the police, comes from 'copper' (policeman) becoming 'grass hopper'.

Some of the rhyming slang Cockneys used has entered the mainstream language. The phrase 'to use your loaf' comes from the cockney 'loaf of bread' which meant 'head'. There were, of course, some unrepeatable ones. 'Tom tit' was one of the least objectionable. But if you call someone a 'berk' you are, I'm afraid, unwittingly referring to the Berkeley Hunt.

r a home prepared
ditional cockney
sh serve saveloys
th pease pudding.

Saveloys

I have never made a saveloy – first, because the ones I have
bought have always been very good and second, because they
would be very difficult to make. But if you have a home
smoker, remember they are just smoked pork sausages. Paul
Corrigan, the famous sausage maker, told me he uses twelve
pounds of lean pork, three pounds of pork fat, five pounds of
rusk (breadcrumbs to you!) moistened with stock and spiced
with salt, pepper, ginger, mace and cinnamon, put into their
cases and lightly smoked for half an hour. That sounds good
enough for me.

Saveloys are delicious by themselves or served with a plate
of bread and butter. Many fish and chip shops offer them as an
alternative or an addition to fish and chips. If you buy them,
steam them for ten minutes and serve them with mustard and
white bread and butter.

oad in the Hole

he schoolboys favourite – and cockneys loved it too! Basically,
is sausages cooked in a Yorkshire pudding. So make a batter,
t the sausages with very hot fat in a baking dish, pour in the
atter and cook in a hot oven until both pudding and sausages
e brown and crisp, say thirty to forty minutes.

You don't know how to make a batter? Where were you
ought up?

You sieve four ounces of flour and a pinch of salt into a basin.
ou make a hole in the middle of the flour and drop in two eggs.
ou beat these in, adding enough milk and water (fifty-fifty)
til you get a good thinnish batter. Now let it rest for at least
alf an hour. The two essentials are very hot fat (but not too
uch of it) and a good hot oven.

hen the Duchess of
rk saw an early
py of this book, she
ld us that Bangers
d Mash was her
vourite dish.

Bangers and Mash

Another childishly simple classic. Fried sausages with mashed
potatoes. Here's the recipe. Fry sausages, mash boiled potatoes.
Serve together.

But there are some tricks and refinements. I always use top
quality pork sausages and I fry them so quickly and in a frying
pan so hot that they burst. (I don't prick them first). Then all
the burst-out bits get crisp and brown. And I add lots of butter,
the top of the milk and a pinch of salt to the mashed potatoes. I
fry and slightly burn onions together with the sausages and if I
have it, some leftover gravy.

Did you know that some people used to use steak, kidneys,
lamb, mushrooms or even oysters instead of sausages?
Barbarians!

Jellies and Marmalade

No one knows when these simple but classic preserves were first made but their origins certainly go way back into medieval times. For the cockney housewife the recipes were never written down but she would know that a pound of sugar to a pint of juice was about right. The fruit was free and the sugar was cheap, so it was an excellent way of keeping the family well fed and satisfying their notorious sweet tooth. The sudden and seasonable glut of Seville oranges would not have gone unnoticed either and, again, a cheap and nourishing preserve could be quickly and expertly made.

A Day in the Country

Once a year, a cockney family would usually manage a day in the country, always on a Sunday and by a cheap excursion rail ticket, by charabanc (coach) or their own 'little donkey shay' – the little donkey-drawn cart the costermonger used for his trade. The time would be late September and each family would know exactly where they were going and what they were going to do.

They were going 'blackberrying', collecting the ripe wild blackberries from the great sheaves of prickly brambles that lined the roads of their familiar part of Kent, Middlesex or Essex. All of them knew 'a best place' and its location was handed down from generation to generation. Mum and Dad would collect the fruit on high while the kids did likewise below. Within a few hours the pots and pans they brought with them would be full of ripe and squashy blackberries and, if there were a few scratched young arms and legs, well, a dab of witch hazel and the promise of a toffee apple would soon take care of that.

The other wild fruit the Cockneys would gather would be crab apples and they would know where the little trees with their harvest of hard, sour little apples could be found. These too would be visited at the appropriate time and their harvest of windfalls carefully collected.

The cockney day in the country combined a good healthy outing with the promise of pounds and pounds of delicious bramble and crab apple jelly. These simple preserves remain among the most delicate and rewarding dishes of Britain.

Marmalade

There were, of course, so many recipes as there were households. Here is a good standard one.

Quarter Seville oranges, take out the pips, put in a saucepan, cover with water, bring to the boil and simmer for an hour. Let cool and chop as you fancy, thick if you like your marmalade like that, or thinly if you prefer it, put the pips in a little cloth bag, and add it to the chopped oranges. Add the water in which they were cooked and weigh. Add a pound and a half of sugar to every pound of pulp. Bring to the boil and simmer for an hour or until the peel is transparent. Remove the bag of pips, pour into hot dry jars and cover. Keep for at least a fortnight, preferably longer.

Crab Apple Jelly

Cut out any damaged and soft parts but otherwise leave the little apples whole. Put them into a pan with enough water to cover them, bring to the boil and simmer until the apples break up into pulp. You can help this process by crushing them against the side of the pan with a wooden spoon. Make a bag from an old tea-towel or sheet, pour the pulp into it, tying the neck with string and handing it where it can strain into a bowl. Do not try to force the juice through or the jelly will be cloudy. Measure the strained liquid, put into a saucepan and bring it to the boil. Add a pound of sugar to each pint of juice and simmer until it sets. Pour into hot dry jars and cover.

Your jam is at 'setting point' when a drop put on a cold plate sets, if it does not, simmer a little longer, stirring all the time.

Bramble Jelly

Gather wild blackberries. If some are a bit squashy and others a bit green, it does not matter – the jelly will be both richer and will set better. Put them in a saucepan with just enough water to prevent burning – half a cupful – and quickly bring to the boil. Reduce the heat and simmer for an hour. From time to time crush the berries against the side of the pan with a wooden spoon to release all the juice.

Make a thick sieve by folding an old tea-towel double and use it to line a colander. Stand the colander in a large pan and carefully pour the juice through it. On no account attempt to force the juice through or the final jelly will be cloudy; let it drain through in its own sweet time.

When all the juice is through – I always leave mine overnight – measure the liquid. Bring it to the boil and then add a pound of sugar to every pint. Keep boiling it until it thickens. Once it reaches 'setting point', pour it into hot dry jars and cover.

Something for Tea

When I was a child we used to sing at school "Do you know the muffin man, do you know the muffin man, who lived down Drury Lane?" The last muffin man must have been dead for decades and none of us had the remotest idea of what he might have looked like. Yet with a cloth-covered board of muffins on his head, ringing his bell and crying his wares, he was once one of the most familiar figures on London's streets.

The gingerbread seller with his board of spicy little cakes would be another welcome visitor.

Cockney Street Cries

Shops only began to appear in any numbers in the streets of London in the second half of the 19th Century. Before then, the needs of East Enders were very largely met by itinerant vendors, who plied their trade from barrows, trays and baskets. Each of them had his or her own individual street cry, and many of them such as 'Cherry ripe! Cherry ripe!' have come down to us in song.

But at the time, the narrow streets of the Cockneys' domain rang to dozens of street cries. 'Muffins! Hot muffins!', 'Old chairs to mend!', 'New Wall Fleet oysters!', 'Long thread laces, long and strong!', 'Buy any four ropes of hard onions!', 'Knives or scissors to grind!', 'Buy my flounders!', 'Hot baked wardens!' (stewed pears), 'Old rare shoes!' and 'Old clothes! Old clothes!' (he would be buying not selling).

A famous music hall song, 'Any old iron! Any old iron!', immortalised one street cry. But today the last relic of the Cockneys' long forgotten street cries must surely be the bell and shout of the rag and bone man. And today he almost certainly shouts from an old van or lorry.

If you ask for a muffin in America you will be served something very different. It is what the Cockney would call a small cake.

Muffins

I don't suppose many Cockneys knew how to begin to make muffins but because they were such a popular item of their diet, I'll give you the recipe anyway.

You will need two pounds of plain flour, a good pinch of salt, an ounce of yeast and enough blood-heat milk to make a soft dough. Cover this and let it rise. Flour your hands and shape the dough into bun-sized pieces. Bake these on a hotplate or preferably, a girdle if you've got one. (The girdle, for those who don't know, is the King Alfred, not the Miss Selfridge model. That is to say, a thick flat iron plate—a girdle—or griddle if you prefer the word), until the muffins are light brown on both sides.

To serve them in the traditional way, break them in half horizontally – this should be easy if you've baked them properly – and toast both halves on both sides. Spread the inside surfaces of both with lots of butter and serve while piping hot.

Gingerbread

Put a pound of flour into a mixing bowl, add ten ounces of black treacle or molasses, two ounces of melted butter, half an ounce of ginger (or less if you like it less gingery), a teaspoonful of bicarbonate of soda and a good pinch of salt. Mix these to a stiff paste, pour into a baking dish and bake in a hot oven (Mark 5) for about half an hour or until a skewer stuck into the centre of the cake comes out clean. Many people think this cake improves with keeping for a couple of days.

I have missed one important instruction. Don't try to weigh the treacle by pouring it into the pan of the scales. Not only will you get the treacle into the mixing bowl but you'll get it everywhere else!

The trick is to heat a small mixing bowl, weigh it and then pour in the treacle until ten ounces more appear on the scales. Then pour the melted and runny treacle into the flour.

If you have the time, inclination and children, you can always make gingerbread men with this recipe. I always allowed my own children to make their own gingerbread men.

Tarts

Cockneys of all ages had a sweet tooth and open tarts are not only sweet but also simple to make, look attractive and taste even better. They also offered an opportunity to make use of the cheap fruit of the season, apples, plums, rhubarb or any odd fruit that 'fell off a barrow'. So, depending on the time of the year, apple tarts, plum tarts, cherry tarts, jam tarts (although these were often made in large quantities of small individual tarts), or rhubarb tarts would be baked and eagerly consumed. Two other favourites, which could be made at any time, were treacle tarts and custard tarts.

Mudlarks

School was not popular with cockney children – nor with their parents. Time at school was time not earning a living and helping the family survive. But there was a limit to what children could do.

One particular job they were very good at because they were light, had good eyesight and were nimble on their feet, was mudlarking.

Mudlarking was gathering treasure from the Thames when the tide was out. This revealed extensive mudbanks that could be searched. At the time, the Thames was London's biggest sewer because it was not until 1859 that the civil engineer, Joseph Bazalgette, started to construct his mighty system of sewers (still in use). Hundreds of sewers delivered their burden directly into London's river. Along with it came objects of some small value. Mudlarks gathered these from the stinking mud and took them home to be cleaned for sale. It could not have been pleasant work. Even so, there was fierce competition for the most rewarding stretches of Thames mud. And occasionally, very occasionally, some small urchin would be rewarded by finding a sovereign, a watch or a valuable piece of jewellery. It was even more occasionally, that these were ever restored to their careless, but rightful, owners.

Nothing would have pleased a cold and shivering mudlark more than to have returned home with his hands full of treasure and be greeted by his anxious cockney mother and a slice of his favourite fruit tart.

Treacle Tart

Rub three ounces of butter and four of lard into half a pound of flour to which has been added a pinch of salt and a teaspoon of baking powder. Moisten this mixture with a little water to bind it. Roll out about a quarter of an inch thick and line a pie dish with this pastry. Keep a little pastry back for decoration. Mix together two heaped tablespoons of fresh white breadcrumbs with a grating of lemon rind and a squeeze of lemon juice and four large tablespoons of golden syrup or golden syrup mixed with black treacle, the proportions depending on how treacly you like the flavour. Fill this into the pastry case and decorate with criss-cross strips of the leftover pastry. Bake in a medium oven for about half an hour.

Custard Tart

For the filling you will need one whole egg plus two yolks, an ounce of sugar and a tablespoonful of flour or less, plus half a pint of creamy milk and half an ounce of melted butter. Mix the egg, yolks, flour and sugar, then add the milk and butter. Line a pie dish with short crust pastry and pour in the mixture. Cook in a hot oven for half an hour. This should produce a surface deliciously decorated with little brown spots. This lovely tart can be eaten hot or cold. It is excellent either way but custard tarts must be eaten within a day of cooking.

Jam Tart

Easy. Line a pie dish with short crust pastry, pour in the jam of your choice (in my own family's case, the jam they wouldn't eat any other way) and bake as for custard tart. It doesn't matter if the jam gets slightly burnt as this produces a crackly, treacly flavour which is much sought after. The children can decorate this tart before cooking with the bits of left over pastry.

Any fruit in season can be used in an open tart – you can use the most exotic fruits although such an unfamiliar choice would make the old East Ender blink in wonder.

Colonial Food

One of the most rewarding
consequences of the British Empire –
even for hard-up Cockneys – was the
large quantities of cheap food imported
from the colonies. The readily
availability of exotic produce such as
mango chutney, is an example of this.
But generations of cockney children
underwent the ordeal of bland, starchy
puddings which filled and fattened them
because they were so cheap, so easy to
prepare and so nutritious. Today we can
enjoy them because they are, in fact,
delicious when they are properly and
carefully prepared.

Uncles

'Uncles' was the polite way the Cockneys described the local pawnbroker, a key
figure in many of their lives. He was the man – or rarely she was the woman –
who kept the cockney family going from mid-week, when the money ran out, to
the weekend when he would be paid, plus a little interest, and the goods
redeemed.

The pattern was that luxury goods – the clock, the best, and all too often, only,
suit or dress, the wedding ring – went first. The unnecessary necessities next –
the carpet, the teacups and saucers, the bedsheets, and finally what was left that
the pawnbroker would be prepared to accept.

The pawnbroker was never a popular figure but the fact remains that often he
was the only intermediary person between a cockney family and real hunger.
Pawned possessions often paid for a desperately needed dinner.

You entered through a sidedoor and into a private booth with a wooden
counter. Discretion was always preserved.

Some 'Uncles' had a Heath-Robinson method of recording the transaction. He
needed one receipt for the customer, one to pin to the goods and one for his own
records. For this he had three pens clasped together and a mechanical arm which,
by moving the pens simultaneously, wrote all three copies at once.

Pawnbrokers are reappearing and going up market. They have even been
known to accept a Porsche as a pledge!

Sago Pudding

Although it was a very bland and not particularly relished by cockney children, who preferred sweeter and textured food, it was undoubtedly good for them – as cockney mothers would have insisted. A very little sago goes a long way because it is very absorbent.

Simply add three heaped tablespoons of sago to a quart of milk, sweeten with a couple of tablespoons of sugar, add a sprinkle of nutmeg and bake for a couple of hours, or until the surface is nicely browned. For myself, I always add a twist of lemon peel to the milk: it improves the flavour.

Sago pudding is now coming back into flavour. Packets of sago can now usually be found on supermarket shelves. There is even a canned version!

Milk Puddings

Tapioca and semolina were two popular milk puddings served instead of sago. Tapioca is a close relative of sago and comes from the same part of the world. Semolina is, in fact, the bits of milled grain that are left after sago flour is sifted at the mill. Both are about as absorbent as sago. Both make the same kind of pudding in the same kind of way.

Rice Pudding

Pour a pint of milk into a pie dish, add six ounces of rice (preferably short grain rice), an ounce or two of sugar, depending on how sweet you want it, and sprinkle the surface with grated nutmeg. Add a knob of butter and put in a medium oven for ninety minutes. Check that it has developed a nice brown skin. If not, turn up the cooker for ten minutes until it has. For cockney kids, this crispy brown skin was the best part of all.

Ground Rice

This is rice ground to a powder. It makes a pudding with the same kind of taste but a quite different texture to a rice pudding – creamier, smoother, blander. But you use exactly the same quantities in exactly the same way. Ground rice pudding should also have a nice brown skin.

Curries

The modern growth of Indian restaurants has developed our taste for Indian cuisine. But long before our time the British used curry powder in their own cooking. By the beginning of the 19th Century English town dwellers were used to the taste of curried food. The Cockneys were no exception. They used curry for the same reason as their Indian contemporaries: neither had refrigerators!

Curry is credited with antiseptic and preservative properties. It certainly made ingredients that were beginning to go off more palatable and added zest to otherwise mundane meals. The use of curry powder met the Cockneys' taste for strong flavours. However, they never went to fashionable classes on Indian cooking. They added curry powder to flavour their own familiar dishes.

Stage Cockneys

Stage Cockneys are frequent secondary characters in plays and films. Portrayed in a patronizing way as cocky, cheerful, ill educated and not very bright. More serious writers like Bernard Shaw in his play *Pygmalion*, upon which the musical *My Fair Lady* was based, created the cockney characters of Eliza Dolittle and her father to show that the only real distinction between the classes was accent and etiquette.

Perhaps the most loved fictional Cockney was Alf Garnett. He featured in the TV comedy series *Till Death Us Do Part* set in East End London. This programme focused on Alf, who lived with his long suffering wife locked in a lifeless marriage. Alf, a boozy, betting West Ham supporter embodied every prejudice, as he was hostile to blacks, gays, and foreigners. Overseas versions of the series were sold worldwide. The USA series was called *All in the Family*. Alf was the creation of Johnny Speight; himself a poorly educated Cockney, the son of a docker. The TV critic T.C. Worsley described Alf Garnett as the "embodiment of all the most vulgar and odious prejudices that slop about in the bilges of the national mind".

This is just what Alf's creator intended. Johnny Speight, who decided to write after reading Bernard Shaw, put into Alf Garnett's mouth the prejudices of all bigots. In doing so he hoped the opinions voiced by Alf would sound just as absurd when proclaimed by the suburban middle classes.

Curried Cheese

Fry a chopped onion in a little butter until brown. Add an oz. of flour and 2 rounded teaspoons of curry powder. Slowly stir in ½ a pint of stock (or a tin of chopped tomatoes with a little water) until the sauce thickens. Fold in 8 ounces of cubed or grated cheese, then add an ounce of sultanas or slices from a peeled and cored apple. Stir on a low heat for a few minutes until hot. Today we would expect to serve curry on a bed of long grain rice but it is just as tasty served with baked or mashed potatoes.

Curried Corned Beef Burgers

Fry a small chopped onion in butter until transparent. Stir in a heaped teaspoon of curry powder and cook for two minutes. Add 8 ounces of chopped corned beef, ½ teacup of fresh breadcrumbs and ½ a teaspoon of Worcester sauce. Press into burger shapes or roll into small balls (about 12), brush over with a beaten egg or milk. Coat with crisp breadcrumbs. Heat in an oven or better still grill them.

Once prepared, the burgers can be stored in the fridge until needed. They can also be eaten cold.

Versatile Curry

Keeping money in their purse as long as possible was the shrewd Cockney housewife's aim. That meant little was allowed to go to waste. Curry powder helped using up left over items of cooked meat or poultry.

This is how to make enough curry sauce for two pounds of mixed cooked vegetables, meat or poultry. Gently fry a chopped onion in 1½ oz of butter until soft, then add a small sliced peeled apple and 2 tablespoons of lemon juice and stir in ½ oz of curry powder, simmer for a few minutes. Then add ½ oz. of flour. Stir in ¾ pint of stock, bring to boil, add the other ingredients and simmer for an hour.

More About Kippers

Kippers had a special place in the Cockney's diet. They were cheap, easy to cook and they kept longer than most fish. Kippers have passed into the colourful language of the Cockneys. East End street traders still describe a period of poor takings as kipper days, because trading is flat. Bosses given the nick name 'kipper' by their workers often felt the title was a form of affection. The Cockneys knew better – a kipper was 'a two-faced bastard without any guts'!

Cockney Villains

Every district has its legionary criminals, the most notorious Cockney villains being the twins Reggie and Ronnie Kray. Illicit gambling and extortion were their specialty. But the Krays had competitors, the Richardson brothers. In background the two rival families could not have been more different. The Krays, whose father was a small-time thief, were born in 1933 into a criminal family living in Bethnal Green. The Richardsons were born in the leafy suburbs of South London, the sons of a prosperous businessman. Gang warfare bought matters to a head on 6 March 1966. Ronnie Kray walked into the bar of the East End pub called *The Blind Beggar* and shot dead one of the Richardsons' henchmen. It was over two years before the police had enough evidence to arrest the twins. After one of the Old Bailey's longest trials, the twins were given life imprisonment.

During their reign of crime the twins posed as generous patrons of boys' clubs and local hospitals. There are still older Cockneys who speak with affection about the Krays. "They only threatened and killed their own kind", their supporters argue. "They kept order and had nothing to do with drugs." This sympathy is misplaced. The Krays came near to establishing an American-style crime syndicate. Their non-drug credentials owe much to the fact they were imprisoned before drug trafficking became so lucrative. Their older brother, Charlie Kray, was given 12 years for drug offence in 1997.

Kipper Parcel

Flake 8 oz of kipper fillets and mix with half pound of mashed potatoes. Season. Roll out enough puff pastry to cover a large dinner plate. If you want to avoid making it yourself use 12 to 14 oz from a packet. Pile kipper and potato mixture in centre. Wet edges of pastry and join together to form a square or triangular shape. Brush with beaten egg and bake in centre of a hot oven for about 30 minutes until puffed and golden.

Curried Kipper Salad

Cockneys thought salad – rabbit food – was not seen on many cockney tables, a substantial salad was acceptable to take on picnics or when in the hop fields. This kipper choice was a favourite. Skin 8 oz of kippers fillets and cut into 2-inch strips. Mix 4 tablespoons of mayonnaise or salad cream with a teaspoon of curry powder and a teaspoon of vinegar. Stir in kipper strips and boiled rice (20 oz raw weight). Add up to 8 oz of sliced tomatoes and 2 sliced hard boiled eggs. Pepper but, unless you like plenty, do not salt.

For another versatile dish, leave out the rice and tomatoes and you have an excellent sandwich filling. It was ideal for an East Enders packed lunch.

Baked Kipper in Tomato Sauce

Cook 4 oz of macaroni in boiling, salted water for 5 minutes, drain and put aside. Prepare a sauce by frying a chopped onion in an oz of butter for 3 minutes. Stir in an oz of flour and cook gently for 2 minutes. Add half a pint of chicken, vegetable or fish stock and then add 8 oz of skinned mashed tomatoes (tinned will do fine). Stir in a tablespoon of mustard. Bring to boil and simmer for 4 minutes.

Slice 8 oz of kipper fillets into 1-inch pieces. Layer the partly cooked macaroni, kipper and sauce alternately in a 2-pint (approximately 1-litre) casserole. Finish with a layer of kippers, topped with tomato sauce. Sprinkle with grated cheese and bake in centre of a moderate oven for 40 minutes.

Baked Beans

"She sends her kids off to school with nothing more than baked beans for breakfast" was a criticism levied at many an East End mother. Her critics ought to have known better. The contents of a tin of baked beans have nearly all the nutrition we need. Served by themselves or with vegetable accompaniment they ensure a balanced meal. Baked beans were another tinned food that met Cockney needs. Unopened they kept forever, and they were easy to prepare and cheap. There are endless ways the ingenious East Ender served them.

The Cockney Accent

Actors born outside London find a cockney accent notoriously difficult. Being marked out as an East Ender might have enhanced one's reputation as a colorful character but it did little to advance social mobility.

A Scottish accent was quite acceptable among doctors and lawyers and though a businessman's Yorkshire accent might be acceptable, a cockney barrister could expect few briefs. Until the sixties, middle class teachers ambitious for their pupils, would do their best to iron out the more obvious Cockney intonations especially the dropped "H".

East End kids were made to recite *It is not the hunting on the hills that hurts the horse's hooves but the hammer on the hard high way.* All too often the verse became *it aint the 'unting on the 'ills.*

For all but the most aspiring children it was a waste of time. They may have spoke 'posh' at school but at home and among their peers the cockney accent prevailed. Overcome the dropped 'H' and the elocutionist had to then tackle the silent T: 'water' became 'war-er'; and the 'V' replaced 'Th', 'bother' became 'bovver'. The sad truth is that a cockney accent is as difficult for the East Ender to drop as it is for the non-cockney actor to acquire.

Hearty Bean Breakfast

A great boost to face a cold morning and nothing could be simpler. Grill or fry 8 ounces of streaky bacon, when cooked cut into half-inch pieces. Empty 2 cans of baked beans into a saucepan add the bacon pieces and heat. While the beans are heating butter four pieces of toast. Serve the hot beans on the toast and top with two sliced hard-boiled eggs.

Family Bean Bake

Fry a chopped onion in a tablespoon of butter or oil until soft. Add a tablespoon of flour and stir in a can of tomatoes and a can of baked beans. Salt, pepper and add a teaspoon of Worcester Sauce and a teaspoon of mixed herbs. Bring to boil. Stir in a pound of diced cooked ham and slices from a large cored and peeled apple. Simmer for 20 minutes stirring occasionally.

Bean and Potato Pie

Fry a chopped onion until tender, add ½ pound of mince meat and cook for 10 minutes then fold in a can of baked beans, season and add a pinch of mixed herbs if you wish. Grease a pie dish, an 8-inch would do fine. Put a pound of mashed potatoes add the bean and meat sauce, top with a further pound of mashed potatoes. Fork the top. Bake in a medium oven for 30 minutes or until the top has started to brown.

Mushrooms were expensive and did not often feature in a cockney diet but today's East Enders might well add 2 ounces of sliced mushrooms to the minced meat. A teaspoon of curry – more if you want it hot – can be added to the mince.

Full of Beans

There must be as many ways of serving beans, as there are beans in a tin. The old East End cafés – never the most imaginative caterers – served baked beans on toast and beans as accompaniment to bacon and eggs. At home the Cockneys were, and still are, more imaginative. Cold they go well with cooked meats, salads and with a hunk of bread, cheese and pickled onions. Try them hot with a baked potato, topped with grated cheese.

East End Kosher

The Jews who escaped to England from the pogroms in Eastern Europe came with nothing but the few miserable possessions that their persecutors had allowed them to keep. But they brought knowledge of one of the world's most remarkable cuisines. So although they were poor, they knew exactly how to prepare the cheap and simple foods that were available to them. Many of these dishes, some slightly refined these days, still find their place on the tables of families now far removed in place and prosperity from their poor and humble forebears of the East End.

The Jewish Cockneys

The infamous pogroms brought successive waves of Jewish immigrants to Britain. The poorest of these came the cheapest way, by cattle boat, and they landed at Britain's least glamorous entry, London Docks. Because they were poor and with few resources, they tended to settle close to their point of arrival and soon there were whole streets where every shop was Jewish. The Yiddish theatre flourished, and there were special schools where dedicated British Jews taught their continental brothers the morals and manners of their new home. There were many small synagogues.

All this has gone now. The shops where Cohen and Klien once flourished have now been taken over by a later wave of immigrants. The old Yiddish theatre is a bingo hall and the synagogues are now Bengali temples. By hard work, intelligence and skill, the cockney Jews have prospered and moved out of their first poor homes.

But for the first two generations the cockney Jews were a close society inside a closed society. Very few of them were ever fully accepted into cockney society and, to be fair to them, very few wanted to be. This did not prevent cultural exchanges. The younger Jews spoke with cockney accents and the native cockney added colourful Jewish expressions to his language such as, "I need him like I need a hole in the head".

Sprouts and Chestnuts

An excellent combination! Trim and wash the sprouts in cold salt water. Drop the chestnuts in boiling water and take out one by one to peel. They peel easily this way, you will soon get the hang of it without burning your fingers. To every pound of trimmed sprouts you will need half a pound of peeled chestnuts. Boil both separately in salted water until tender – the chestnuts will take longer.

Blooms, famous for its salt beef, was a World famous Jewish restaurant in Whitechapel, the heart of London's East End. Strictly kosher, neither its customers, nor its staff, however, were strictly Jewish. It used to be said of Blooms that you could ask any Jew anywhere in the world to meet you there, it was so well known. Unfortunately, it closed in 1996.

Motza Appetiser

Jewish cockney children loved this – and still do. You simply rub Motzas with a raw onion, sprinkle this with salt, dry them in the oven for a couple of minutes, spread dripping on them and serve hot. These were often cooked on the lower shelf of the oven while potatoes were being baked on the upper shelves. You served the crisp and tasty motzas as an appetiser to the potatoes, which were eaten later.

Mashed Turnips

For this delicious way of serving turnips, you'll need a pound
of them, pepper, salt and fat. Wash, peel and slice the turnips,
put them in a saucepan, cover with water, bring to the boil and
simmer until the turnips are soft. Strain off the water, add the
pepper and salt and an ounce of the fat of your choice – I find
beef dripping is just about perfect for this dish. Put the mashed
turnips in a greased oven-proof dish and heat in a very hot oven
for ten minutes. Using swedes, the Scots serve this with haggis
as 'bashed neeps'.

Salt Cucumbers

These traditional delicacies, known in the East End as 'wallies',
soon escaped from the Jewish kitchen and quickly found their
way into the fish and chip shops of the East End. Now they have
become a national dish all over the country.

   Salt cucumbers were originally prepared only in small wooden
barrels and, my Jewish friends tell me, they only taste proper
when made this way. Could be – but as I have no small wooden
barrel I have to use a crock. Best for this pickle are ripe, ridge
cucumbers – the squat, knobbly ones. Soak them in water for
twelve hours (this gets them spongy and absorbent) and lay them
lengthways in the crock with a handful of peppercorns, and four
bay leaves and – if you can get them – vine and cherry leaves.
Boil water, adding a teaspoon of salt to each pint. Let this cool
and pour over the cucumbers, just covering them. Cover the
crock and leave for a fortnight when the cucumber will be ready
to eat. Traditionally, the wooden barrel is left in the garden sun
for this time, with the barrel being turned from time to time. In
this country? You must be joking!

Shabbas Soup

Traditional for Sabbath lunches, cheap, tasty and nourishing.
Take half a pint of haricot beans, half a pint of coarse barley,
add a piece of fatty meat and a marrow bone. Put these into a
casserole with five pints of water, add pepper and salt, and, as
pious Jewish families did, put the casserole in a low oven and
leave it to cook all night.

Tomato Soup and Einlauf

This is the Jewish version of vegetable stew and dumplings. It's a bit rough and ready so you can alter the proportion of vegetables as you like – so long as tomatoes predominate. For a typical soup, use a pound of pot-herbs – swedes, turnips, parsnips, carrots – and two pounds of tomatoes, three ounces of sago, salt and pepper and three pints of water.

Cook the sago for an hour in half a pint of water. Chop all the vegetables and tomatoes, season with the pepper and salt, put them into the water in a saucepan and bring to the boil. Now add the sago and water and cook gently for ninety minutes.

For the einla'uf (dumplings) take three tablespoonsful of flour, an egg, a quarter of a cup of water and a pinch of salt. Mix all together to a smooth paste. Take spoonfuls of this and drop them gently into the hot soup. They'll solidify in no time at all. Serve piping hot. Shalom!

Brown Fish Stew

This alarming sounding dish is always served cold. It has a strange taste – but one you will want to return to, believe me.

You'll need three onions, three pounds of mixed fish (any will do) two small gingerbread cakes, three quarters of a cup of vinegar, six ounces of treacle, a sliced lemon, chopped parsley and pepper and salt – plus half a pint of cold water.

Peel and slice the onions and cook in a large saucepan with the water until they are soft. Add the fish and the seasoning and cook gently for half an hour. Crumble the gingerbread cakes into the vinegar and mix in the treacle. Pour all this in with the fish (be brave!) and cook for another quarter of an hour.

Let cool and put the fish into a shallow dish or dishes. Serve cold, garnished with slices of lemon and chopped parsley. As I said, once you've got used to it you'll want it again, and again, and again.

Chrine

This splendid relish is traditionally served with meat dishes, hot or cold. I also eat it with cheese, with cold fish and with vegetarian dishes. Simply, you grate horseradish (watch your eyes!) and beetroot finely together, mix in a pinch of salt and a little sugar and add white vinegar to taste. It looks good, it tastes good, it is good!

Solid Fare

Like all careful housewives, cockney mothers would eke out expensive meat dishes with plenty of solid and substantial accompaniments – potatoes, dumplings, Yorkshire pudding. This 'belly timber' would fill the corner of hungry kids – and their dads too. But it had to be nice and tasty as well as sustaining and nutritious.

Boiled Beef

Very few of the old music hall songs have survived from their heyday a century ago but at 'knees-ups', where the over 60's are in a majority, you will still hear one or two of the old songs that are belted out with gusto, among them, of course, is 'Boiled Beef and Carrots'. Most of the words would have been well understood by an Edwardian audience but for the ill-educated modern reader the words 'Derby Kell' are a shortened version of 'Derby Kelly', rhyming slang for 'Belly'.

Verse

When I was a nip-per on-ly six months old, my mo-ther and my fa-ther too,
They didn't know what to wean me on, They were both in a dread-ful stew;
They thought of tripe, they thought of steak, Or a bit of old cod's roe,
I said, I'm round to the old cook-shop, I know what'll make me grow.

Chorus

Boiled beef and carrots, That's the stuff for your 'Dar-by kel', makes you fat and it keeps you well,
Don't live like a veg-e-tar-i-ans, On food they give to par-rots,
From morn till night, blow out your kite on boiled beef and carrots.

Boiled Beef

It's not surprising that the most famous of all cockney dishes, boiled beef and carrots, had its own anthem, roared out in every music hall. Salt silverside was the usual joint, but brisket and topside were also very popular.

To make boiled beef and carrots, soak the joint overnight, throw away the water and put the beef in a big saucepan, covering it with fresh water and adding a bay leaf, a sprig of parsley, a handful of peppercorns and a clove stuck into an onion. For every pound of meat, scrape a pound of carrots to add during the last hour of cooking. Bring to the boil and simmer an hour, or until the beef is tender. I always add dumplings too. They make the meat go further.

Dumplings

Heavy as lead, as big as your fist, these were the cockney housewife's ammunition against the appetites of hungry families.

Use half a pound of self-raising flour (or plain flour with a teaspoon of baking powder), four ounces of shredded or grated suet, a cup or so of cold water and a pinch of salt. Mix them all to make a soft dough, roll them in your hands to make small – but not too small – balls. Drop into the boiling liquid twenty minutes before you are due to serve. Wonderful belly-cheaters or timber!

Pease Pudding

A nutritious and satisfying dish, familiar to mediaeval peasants, all over Europe. Cockney eating-houses always had a large bowl of it. There are hundreds of ways of preparing this simple dish but this is the way many cockney mothers cooked it.

Using lentils rather than split peas, soak overnight and simmer for a couple of hours in plenty of water with a meaty ham-bone. Drain them, saving the water, mash thoroughly, add a knob of butter, pepper and salt. Tie this mixture into a cloth and re-boil in the original water (with more added, if necessary) for another hour. Serve hot. I have always eaten this with a cheap bacon joint which I substitute for the ham-bone. The two go together perfectly.

Festive Fare

Cockneys always liked a 'blow-out'
whether it was a wedding, someone's
birthday, a golden wedding or a funeral.
They liked plenty to eat and drink,
almost any excuse would do. Easter and
Christmas were obvious occasions to
celebrate and there would always be
something good and tasty to hand.

Christmas was especially favoured.
The East End shops and stalls would be
decorated with tinsel and holly, with the
butchers' shops full of turkeys and pork
joints, and the costermonger's stalls
piled high with oranges, tangerines and
nuts.

Christmas

The meagre Christmas so vividly described by Dickens in *A Christmas Carol*
would have been all too familiar to many cockney families. But however poor,
the mums would always manage to produce something special and tasty for
Christmas dinner, even if it was only a small piece of pork with crackling. There
would always have been a Christmas Pudding.

The Cockney mum would go to great lengths to see the children had some
sweets on the day. She would have saved a few pence through the year to make
sure that every one of her children had a stick of barley sugar, a sugar mouse and
an orange in their Christmas stocking so eagerly left out the night before. I well
remember the sugar mouse and the orange in my own Christmas stocking. Alas,
sugar mice seem to have disappeared.

We are all familiar with Christmas left-overs, turkey sandwiches and even
turkey curries, which in the days of refrigerators can be on the menu on the
twelfth day of Christmas. The same opportunities were not available to the
Cockneys but Christmas Pudding kept well. That is why the shrewd cockney
mother would always ensure that there was enough Christmas Pudding for her old
man to take to work for the days after Christmas.

Mince Pies

A must for Christmas, then and now. You'll need short pastry,
mincemeat and a little caster sugar for dusting the finished
pies. Cut out circles of pastry, one bigger than the other. Place
the bigger circles of pastry into a patty dish. Fill them
generously with mincemeat and cover with smaller circles of
pastry. Bake in a medium oven for half an hour. Dust with
caster sugar. Mince pies are, of course, perfectly acceptable
cold, but how much better hot, preferably so hot that they burn
your tongue!

Stuffed Dates

The familiar oblong packets of sticky dried dates from Egypt or other North African countries made their appearance in the East End shops late in the 19ᵗʰ Century and soon became a familiar if not essential part of a cockney Christmas.

In my family, it was the children's responsibility to take the dates out of the box, dip them in caster sugar, split them with a blunt knife, remove the stone and insert a blanched almond. There was much agreeable licking of sticky fingers! These titbits were served to pacify infants' appetites when we all thought the turkey would never be ready.

Roast Chestnuts

About Christmas, the roast chestnut sellers would appear on the streets of the East End. Their equipment was a glowing coke fire in the bottom of an old oil drum or something similar, a pierced metal grid, often the lid of the oil drum, punched full of holes and lots of little paper bags to sell the 'penn'oth' of roast chestnuts in. They simply put the chestnuts on the grid and cooked them until the skin was partially blackened. They never forgot to lightly slash the skin first to stop them unprofitably exploding – and so should you to save your carpets. Cooked this way they have a special taste all of their own.

You can reproduce the effect by putting your slashed chestnut on a shovel and heating it over a coal or wood fire. Being so hot when they are freshly cooked, they are difficult to peel. Burnt tongues are not unknown.

Lemonade

When lemons were cheap and in season, cockney mums would prepare a refreshing summer drink in some quantities. She would carefully peel the lemons so that no pith was left on the peel (pith makes the final lemonade bitter). She would put this peel in a jug and cover it with boiling water.

The peeled lemons would then be squeezed and all the juice extracted, discarding the pips which, like the pith, make the lemonade bitter. She would add sugar to taste, about an ounce per lemon, and pour on boiling water, half a pint per lemon or so, depending on the size of the lemon. She would mix this with the peel water and, after removing the peel, allow to cool, and bottle – it was ready to drink diluted with as much cold water as your taste required.

Ginger-Beer

This was a splendid treat for cockney children. Their mums would have used dry root ginger, but you can use the real fresh root now widely available.

Take the carefully peeled rinds of three lemons. Smash half a pound of fresh ginger until it begins to break up. Put the rinds, the ginger, two pounds of sugar and two ounces of cream of tartar into a big pot and pour on two and a half gallons of boiling water. Let it cool until the liquid is lukewarm and add two tablespoonsful of yeast, either fresh or dried. Let it all cool and stand for twelve hours. Add the lemon juice, strain and bottle tightly. It will be splendidly fizzy in a couple of days.

Christmas Pudding

Everyone has their own favourite recipe for Christmas Pudding and so long as there is more fruit than all the other ingredients put together, I don't suppose it matters very much which one you use. This is one which I believe would come closest to what a cockney mum would have given her family.

Mix together half a pound of currants, three quarters of a pound each of sultanas and stoned raisins, half a pound of brown sugar, half a pound each of self-raising flour and fresh breadcrumbs, six well-beaten eggs, the grated rind and juice of an orange and a lemon, a teaspoon each of salt and mixed spice, six ounces of finely chopped apple, a quarter of a pound each of chopped candied peel and glace cherries, a finely chopped carrot, six ounces of chopped blanched almond and a wine glass of brandy. Mix well moistening with a little brown ale if the mixture is too stiff.

Put the mixture into a basin, cover tightly with foil or floured cloth and boil for eight hours, making sure the water doesn't boil dry. Store in a cool, dry place and steam for three hours before serving.

Fudge

For more sophisticated palates add coffee powder, cocoa or walnuts. Only put these in when you have taken the mixture from the cooker.

Here is a simple basic recipe. For every pound of sugar take six ounces of evaporated milk, a quarter of a pint of water and three ounces of butter. Put ingredients into a heavy saucepan and bring to boil. Stirring all the time, gently boil until the mixture begins to thicken (about 15 minutes).

Place saucepan on a cool surface (a metal draining board is ideal) and stir with a wooden spoon until mixture is thick and creamy. Then pour into a buttered dish. When firm, cut with a sharp serrated knife.

Hard Times

For the comparatively well-off
Cockneys – bookmakers, owners of
several market stalls, publicans and
card-sharpers – life could be very
pleasant indeed. For middle-range
East Enders, never noted for their
farsightedness, life was a bit of a
struggle and the popular loan clubs
were a useful insurance against
expensive demands like holidays,
birthdays and Christmas. For the
very poorest Cockney, life was a
constant losing battle against the rent
man, disintegrating clothing and the
final menace of the workhouse. For
such households, recipes as cheap as
basic vegetable soup or stew-pot were
the difference between life and
starvation

Loan Clubs

'Loan Clubs' were a widespread feature of East End life and were a tribute to
cockney thrift or, more likely, the cockney housewife's thrift. They seem to have
appeared spontaneously. This is how they worked. On the first Monday of the
New Year, two 'collectors' would set up a table in the bar of their local pub and
wait for their clients. When these arrived they would pay in the first of a regular
series of small sums to start their 'card'. They would record this and all
subsequent weekly payments, which would accumulate towards the annual
Christmas 'payout'.

   The saver would be obliged to take out loans throughout the year. These
usually financed holidays, birthdays or some other financial necessity. When these
loans were repaid, the saver paid a small extra sum for the privilege. These small
sums accumulated to generate the interest to provide a Christmas bonus for each
saver – minus a small sum called 'House money' which had to be spent in the
pub. This was good news for the saver and the publican.

   The 'collectors' were obviously men who were widely trusted by the East End
clients and it would be nice to say that they never betrayed this trust. Alas, it was
not uncommon for 'burglaries' or 'robberies' to take place shortly before the
Christmas payout, where the poor unfortunate collector was relieved of all his
clients' savings!

Stew-pot

This must surely be one of the first dishes ever conceived by man. It is a universal recipe where food and resources are scarce and have to be carefully husbanded: it was as familiar to the ancient Egyptian peasant as it is to his modern French counterpart. It played an essential part in the lives of many of the poorest Cockneys. It kept them alive from day to day.

Briefly, it is a pot on the top of the stove into which is put anything that is edible and remotely suitable – vegetables, bones, meat scraps, leftovers, cereals – anything that yields a calorie or a vitamin. It would, of course, exclude fish and sweet things but apart from these, almost anything is suitable. The stewpot is kept going for days, weeks, months – and in some well-documented instances – years, constantly visited by the ladle as eating time arrived, constantly replenished with water, seasoning and whatever animal or vegetable matter was to hand. It never got cold, it never emptied.

Of course, the process of continuous cooking fairly soon reduced the contents of the stewpot to an indifferentiated mush, with the texture of watery porridge. But it was sustaining and, sharply seasoned, easy to eat.

I do something similar after Christmas and other heavy eating and drinking times. Only I call it a stockpot – fill it with turkey, chicken, or bones, vegetable scraps, add bay-leaves, onions, garlic, peppercorns and eventually strain it to be frozen into stock cubes. I use it for weeks and months after.

Vegetable Soup

This is the simplest soup of all and familiar to peasants of any nation in the world. All you do is to take any vegetables available, chop them and cook them in water. The less water you cook them in the thicker – and more costly – the soup. Cockney vegetable soup is a reminder to modern cooks that excellent soup can be made without worrying too much about the ingredients or the amounts. Their soups would have contained any combination in any proportion of onions, carrots, turnips, parsnips, swedes, celery, potatoes, peas, beans – you name it, it would have gone in. Plus a little salt.

Today a variation on this basic theme would be served in any vegetarian restaurant and highly valued. Make it at home and it still tastes good – and is good for you, your waistline and your purse.

Those Were the Days

"It's a wery remarkable circumstance", said Sam "that poverty and oysters always seem to go together". Thus the cockney Sam Weller said to Mr Pickwick. However unlikely the combination may seem today, in Dickens's time oysters were both cheap and plentiful. The Thames was full of salmon and cockney apprentices complained about being served it too often. Fashions in food change with its availability; anybody of the pre-war generation can remember when chicken was a rare and expensive treat. It somehow seemed to taste better too.

The fact remains that Cockneys of the early 19th Century took for granted dishes that today grace only the tables of the very rich. I offer a few to show how times have changed.

Music Halls

One of the Cockney's favourite places of entertainment was his local music hall, a cross between a theatre and a pub. Here he could drink his pint of old ale and listen to his favourite artiste singing humorous, patriotic or sentimental songs – 'Any Old Iron', 'Soldiers of the Queen', 'Knocked them in the Old Kent Road' and so on, in which he would loudly join them in the chorus. Some cockney stars went on to become famous national figures – Marie Lloyd, Nellie Wallace, Little Titch, Champagne Charlie (George Leybourne). At least one went on to win international fame – Charlie Chaplin.

Not one music hall remains now, though a good imitation takes place at the Players Theatre near Charing Cross Station. But in their heyday there were hundreds of them. Some of the gentry liked to 'dress down', disguising themselves as working men to visit music halls. Edward VII, when he was Prince of Wales, was a well known incognito visitor to cockney music halls.

Another recipe
verbatim from 'A Plain
Cookbook for the
Working Classes'.

Baked Goose

'Pluck and pick out all the stubble feathers, thoroughly clean,
draw the goose, cut off the head and neck, and also the feet and
wings, which must be scalded to enable you to remove the
pinion feathers from the wings and the rough skin from the feet,
split and scrape the inside of the gizzard and carefully cut out
the gall from the liver. These giblets well stewed, will serve to
make a pie for another day's dinner. Next put six potatoes to
bake in the oven and while they are being baked, chop six
onions with four apples and twelve sage leaves and put these in
a saucepan with two ounces of butter, pepper and six baked
potatoes, and use this very nice stuffing to fill the inside of the
goose. The goose being stuffed, place it upon an iron trivet* in
a baking dish containing peeled potatoes and a few apples; add
half a pint of water, pepper and salt, shake some over the goose
and bake it for almost an hour and a half'.

This sounds rather good! But today it would be very
expensive.

Stewed Oysters

'Put the oysters, with their liquor and a little water or milk,
into a saucepan; add a bit of butter, kneaded that is, well
mixed with a tablespoonful of flour; pepper and a little salt;
stir the oysters over the fire until they have gently boiled for
about five minutes and then pour them into a dish containing
some slices of toasted bread.'

*Trivet would have
been a familiar word
to Victorian readers.
Today we would
describe it as a short
legged stand for pots.

Baked Suckling Pig

'Let the pig be stuffed in the same manner as directed for a
goose, score it all over cropwise, rub some butter upon it, place
it upon a trivet* in a dish containing peeled potatoes and a few
sliced onions, season with pepper and salt; add half a pint of
water and bake the pig for about two hours, basting it
frequently with its own dripping, or a bit of butter tied up in a
piece of muslin'.

Party Fare

Street parties were for children, so the basic foods were jellies, biscuits and cakes. These were often decorated with 'hundreds and thousands' because the children liked the pretty colours. Today parents use 'Smarties' to get the same effect. The whole idea of street party fare is to look cheerful and bright.

Street Parties

Cockneys loved parties – a good 'knees-up' in your own home, a sing-song in the pub on Derby Day or New Year's Eve or a street party, whenever there was an excuse for one.

Street parties were special – and cockney families spent much time and effort in preparing them. Notionally, they were for the kids to celebrate some great national festivity – a Coronation, a Jubilee, the end of a war, a Royal Wedding. I suspect the grown-ups enjoyed them every bit as much as the children – and probably more.

Each family had to provide a table and chairs for the children to sit on. Posh families would show off by providing a tablecloth.

The food followed a pattern. There would be jellies and trifles, cakes and buns and lots of bread and jam. There would be lemonade and fizzy drinks for the children and more substantial drinks for the grown-ups.

There would be games for the children – pass the parcel, musical chairs, forfeits. There would be dancing and a sing-song. Finally stuffed to the gills with jelly and jam, the children would be sent off to bed, the tables and chairs cleared and the adults would begin their half of the street party.

Street parties still take place in the East End – and, of course, elsewhere in London and Britain. But the character has changed. The cockney children's sweet tooth has been replaced by the desire for savoury things – sausages, crisps, fish fingers, ham sandwiches. And these days the grown-ups are drinking gin and tonic, sherry or Bulgarian red wine.

A popular street
party dish was an
assortment of
coloured chopped
jellies served in a
ttle dish or paper
up topped with a
herry or two.

Jellies

To add a bit of cockney colour to your jellies, build them up in
layers using a different flavour and hence a different colour
each time. All you need to do is to follow the manufacturer's
instructions to make the jelly. Fill your dish or mould to a
quarter with one colour jelly. As soon as it sets, fill the next
quarter with jelly of another colour, go on until you have four
colours and the mould is full.

Unlike the old street party organiser, who may have had to
spread the task over two days, a refridgerator can reduce the
time needed to a few hours. An attractive combination was
lime, blackcurrant, lemon and strawberry.

Iced Buns and Cakes

These are simply, cheap, plain buns glazed with icing. Follow
the instructions on the packet to make the icing. Then spread
it thinly over the top of the bun.

This looks nice and satisfies a sweet tooth, but there are
many interesting variations. Sprinkle the icing with 'hundreds
and thousands' before it sets. Or spell out each child's initial
in 'Smarties'. Again, you can colour the icing with the various
vegetable dyes you can buy in any supermarket. Chocolate
icing can be made by incorporating cocoa with the dry icing
sugar.

Broken Biscuit Cake

Supermarkets and chain stores do not sell broken biscuits
although you can sometimes still buy them very cheaply at a
corner grocer. In the past cockney children could buy a
ha'porth of broken biscuits in a 'screw' of newspaper. For
broken biscuit cake their mums would need more substantial
quantities. But still very cheap.

Crush about half a pound of sweet or digestive biscuits (a
mixture of both is fine) with a rolling pin. You will also need
three and a half ounces of butter, two ounces of cocoa, one
ounce of caster sugar, and three ounces of golden syrup.

First cream the butter, sugar and syrup. Then mix in cocoa.
Now add the crushed biscuits and mix well. Press into an 8-in
flan-ring. Leave in a cool place. Once again you can score off
the old Cockneys who had no 'fridge'. Leave over-night,
remove the flan-ring and coat with icing sugar.

Cockney Sweets

Cockney children – like all children – loved sweets. On high days and holidays cockney mothers could sometimes be persuaded by their young families to make sweets. These would be uncomplicated recipes – and none the worse for that. Some of them, like treacle toffee and toffee apples are still widely made, to delight the sweet tooth of youngsters today.

Many of the sweets cockney children bought with their ha'pennies and farthings were manufactured in small local factories and are no longer made by the big conglomerates which now make our sweets. But gobstoppers and liquorice laces can still be found by the discriminating young seeker.

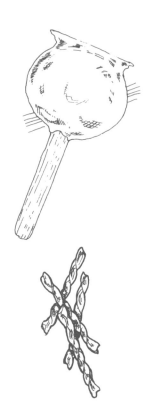

The Cockney Patriots

Famous occasions for street parties were the Relief of Mafeking during the Boer War, the Coronation of Edward VII and George V and VI, the Silver Jubilee of George V and the Coronation of our own Queen Elizabeth II. When George V and Queen Mary visited the East End on their Coronation, they were greeted in one street by the famous banner 'Lousy but Loyal'.

Cockney fervour on these occasions should come as no surprise. The East Ender was always fearlessly loyal. They were the first to enlist and in the 1914-18 war cockney streets were denuded of their men who swarmed to join the colours, ironically afraid that the war would be over before they saw any action. Whole cockney battalions went over to France. Alas, no whole cockney battalions returned.

The East End soldiers were not demobilised in time to attend the street parties which celebrated the end of the war but their families made up for this later by decorating their houses with flags and bunting to greet each returning cockney warrior.

Treacle Toffee

Boil together a pound of demerara sugar, half a pound of butter, half a pound of black treacle and the juice of a lemon. The toffee will be ready when a small drop dropped into cold water becomes hard and brittle at once. When this has happened, pour the toffee into a buttered baking tin or something similar and leave to cool. You will need to break this brittle toffee into pieces with a rolling pin or similar kitchen implement. If you have children around you will have trouble keeping enough of this toffee to store.

Toffee Apples

For this you will need some small, sweet apples, short-pointed sticks, and wooden skewers and a quantity of boiling toffee together with a bowl of ice-cold water.

This toffee should be exactly the same as for the previous recipe but substituting golden syrup for the black treacle.

Pierce the apples firmly with the wooden stick or skewer. Dip them briefly into the boiling toffee mixture and plunge them immediately into the cold water. The toffee will set immediately to form a crisp shell around the apple. The toffee that is left over can be poured into another buttered dish to make straight-forward toffee.

By adding a little colouring to each mix, you can get a variety of different coloured sweets.

Sugar Sticks

The cockney sweet maker would have used a marble cooling slab rubbed with cooking oil. This is not common in the modern refrigerated home, but a large plate will do nearly as well.

For every two pounds of sugar allow one egg white and one pint of water. Dissolve the sugar in the water and gently heat, adding a well-beaten egg white before the mixture gets warm. Stir well, and once the mixture boils remove the scum with a slotted spoon. Once it looks clear, strain through a fine sieve or a cloth bag. Boil again and keep testing by dropping a small amount into a bowl of cold water. As soon as a drop sets immediately, the mixture is ready. Add lemon juice, let the mixture cool for two minutes. Then pour on to the oiled plate or slab. Cut into strips and twist into spirals.

Jellied Meats

Some people love soft, gelatinous, chewy meat – others hate it. Cockneys simply loved it. It was cheap, simply prepared and nourishing. It was, in fact, the despised parts of those animals which were consumed in wealthier households – the discarded heads, feet and innards of the cattle, pigs and sheep whose flesh went into the roasts, steaks and chops of the toffs. In fact this offal, simply prepared, can be tansformed into some of the most delectable dishes in the world. What the Cockneys cheaply enjoyed are served in the very best French restaurants at prices that would ruin you.

A 'Knees-Up'

Cockneys, however poor, were very sociable people and enjoyed nothing more than a good party. Any excuse was good enough for a party – a birth, a marriage, an anniversary, even a death. The women would prepare the food, the brawns, meat pies, cow-heel, and the men would fetch the bottles of porter for the men and stout for the women. They would then all gather at a party-giver's home.

There was always someone who was – or believed themselves to be – a good mimic. He or she would do a turn, imitating one of the popular music-hall stars. There would be a singer who would make them laugh or cry with a humorous or sentimental ballad. Then there would be a communal sing-song. They would all sing popular songs like 'Nellie Dean', 'My Old Dutch' and 'Any Old Iron'. The 'Knees-up' itself, was a dance with much jumping and stamping around an old piano.

A 'Knees-up' is still a feature of London life, no longer confined to the East End. The phrase itself comes from a popular music hall song. What it all actually means, has always been a mystery.

Knees up, Mother Brown, Knees up, Mother Brown
Under the table you must go, E-I-E-I-E-I-O
If I catch you bending, I'll saw your legs right off
Knees up, Knees up, Don't get the breeze up
Knees up, Mother Brown.

Calves Head

This is one of the most creamily gelatinous of all jellied meats and, again, as highly regarded on aristocratic French tables as in a cockney kitchen.

As for all such meat, it is simmered in salted water with an onion, carrot, parsley, peppercorns, a bay-leaf until the flesh leaves the bones. It is then taken from the liquor and either served cold as a sort of brawn or hot, sliced, and accompanied with boiled potatoes. In both cases, a vinaigrette sauce is poured over it (vinegar, oil, pepper, salt and a little mustard mixed together). For myself, I remove the cooked brains and beat them into the vinaigrette to make an extra tasty sauce, but here I depart from cockney orthodoxy.

Brawn

This still remains an amazingly cheap dish to make and enjoy.
There are a number of variations to the basic recipe.

Get your butcher to split a pig's head into half (hopefully he'll
have already removed the eyes). Put the two halves into a large
saucepan, add salt, an onion, a carrot, a few sprigs of parsley, a
handful of peppercorns and a bay-leaf.

Bring to the boil and simmer until the flesh comes away from
the bones easily – about two hours. Let cool, remove the head
from the liquor, take out all the bones and coarsely chop the
remaining flesh, including the tongue and ears.

Put the chopped meat into a large basin and strain the cooking
liquor over. Now I like my brawn fairly soft, so I would leave it
at that. But Cockneys preferred their brawn much firmer, as they
would re-boil the liquor and reduce it by as much as half. This
results in a much stiffer jelly.

I always serve with a sauce made from mustard, brown sugar,
vinegar, cooking oil and a pinch of ground clove. Adjust these
ingredients to your taste.

Trotters

These were great delicacies for the Cockneys and are, again,
very easy to prepare. Check with your butcher whether he has
pre-prepared them for you. If he has, they will need less
cooking.

Put the trotters in a saucepan and cover with water to
which has been added the usual onion, carrot, parsley,
peppercorns, bay leaf and salt. Bring to the boil and simmer
until the flesh is tender and easily pierced: this can take as
little as two hours or as long as four. Take the trotter from the
hot liquor, put into a dish and strain the liquor over. Allow to
cool.

As usual, the Cockney ate his trotter cold with salt, pepper
and vinegar. Jolly good too! But the French have practically a
whole cuisine based on trotters. Just to show you, I'll quote
part of one recipe from Jane Grigson's famous book on
French pork cookery.

"If you intend to breadcrumb and grill the trotters
eventually, or if you intend to stuff them, you must tie the
trotters one on each side of a small flat piece of wood about
two inches wide and eight inches long. Do this by bandaging
them closely and firmly, so that they cannot lose their shape
in the cooking".

That would have made the cockney housewife sit up!

Calves' Feet

These can be prepared in exactly the same way as pigs' trotters but will not need nearly as much simmering as the flesh is much softer. They can also be served in exactly the same way.

Curiously, the Cockneys almost never did. What they would do, would be to overcook the calves feet until the flesh had almost literally dissolved, strain the liquor off, discard the rags of flesh, add a little lemon juice and sugar to the hot liquid and let this cool.

The jelly left was soft, sweet and succulent and was given to sickly children and to invalids as a basic strengthening food. Generations of Jewish mothers have had exactly the same sentiments about chicken soup.

Cowheel

You buy cow heels ready cleaned and split from the butcher. Cockney housewives knew exactly what to do with them. Put the cowheel in a saucepan and cover with water. Add salt, an onion, a carrot, a few sprigs of parsley and a handful of peppercorns (and I add a bay leaf, which the Cockneys would not have done). Bring to the boil and simmer for a couple of hours or until the flesh is easily pierced with a fork.

The East End practice was to lift the cow heel from the hot liquor, put it into a shallow dish and strain the cooking liquor over it. This would then be allowed to cool into a jelly.

The cold jellied cow heel would then be eaten with salt, pepper and vinegar. This remains very good but you can also eat cow heel hot by boning it (the bones should separate very easily if it has been cooked long enough), rolling the flesh – either whole or cut into strips – in breadcrumbs and then grilling it under a hot grill until it turns a delicious brown. Serve this piping hot with English or continental mustard thinned with vinegar. Or, as I prefer, with a creamy horseradish sauce.

Sheep's Trotters

These are never seen now but were a common, cockney delicacy. They were sold clean by the butcher, stewed with peppercorn, a sprig of thyme, a little salt and a wineglass of vinegar, simmered for three hours and served piping hot.

Cockney Kids

The cockney kids soon learned how to survive in the tough life of the East End, helped by an occasional gob-stopper when they got things right and, more often, by a 'clip around the ear' when they got them wrong. They learned to call at the fish and chip shop when the owner would have collected enough little batter pieces to fill a screw of paper – and they would know that if they were 'peaky' their mum would build them up with bread and milk and beef tea.

'Moonlight Flit'

Many East End landlords were absentees – rich men, who rented out their squalid houses to Cockneys at exorbitant rents. These were usually collected by that sinister figure, the 'rent man' who could generally call on powerful 'minders' if his clients became difficult. Small cockney kids learned their trade by telling the rent man the tale while his parents cowered in the back room. Bigger cockney kids were naturally adept at telling the tallest stories with a straight face.

If the Cockney built up a rent debt he simply couldn't pay, he would have to resort to the famous 'moonlight flit'. For this, he would load all his household goods and family onto his own or a borrowed or rented cart and silently remove everything to a newly rented location, leaving no trace behind. To keep his move absolutely silent, the wily Cockney using a donkey and shay would pad the donkey's hooves. His neighbours, who might well need such help themselves sometime, would never, never know that he was going or where he had gone.

Beef Tea

This clear, strong amber broth was taken as much as a medicine as a food and was widely prescribed for both weakly children and the old and feeble. As a hot drink on a cold, wet winter's night it beats brandy any time. For it you need half a pound of shin of beef, a teacupful of water, a pinch of salt – and patience.

Chop the beef into small pieces and put it in a two-pound jam jar with the water. Stand this in a saucepan of water and put it on the lowest possible heat. Cockney mothers would have put it on the back of the stove. Leave overnight or at least twelve hours, adding the salt after it has been gently cooking for six hours. Do not on any account let the saucepan boil dry. Strain, pressing the cooked beef gently to extract all the savoury juice. Cool, taking care to remove any spot of fat that remains. Reheat and serve in a teacup or mug.

Pork Scratchings

You buy these in little packets in pubs these days but any cockney kid could have told you where they came from. When his mum rendered down bits of pork rind to extract the lard or dripping, the hard, succulent crackly bits that were left were very popular with all children. A similar treat was the crisp, fried fragments of batter which fell to the bottom of the deep fryer in the fish and chip shop. When he cleared out his fryer, the fish and chip man would sell these in a screw of paper for a farthing or a halfpenny.

Bread and Milk

We never gave this to our own children, but I remember being given this as a small boy when I was under the weather. All it was, was a slice of bread and butter broken into pieces and dropped in a mug of hot sweet milk. I always felt better for it.

Broth

Another basic. The cheapest bones
from the butcher boiled to rags with a
handful of vegetables. In fact, broth is
very good for you, healthy, tasty and full
of nourishment. It is what smart
cookbooks call 'stock'.

Cockney mothers clearly differentiated
between soup and broth. Soup was thick,
whereas broth was thin and clear.

The London Docks

Samuel Pepys mentioned the London docks in 1691. A fine Roman quay, where
their galleys must have tied up, was discovered during excavations in the 1970's.
The fact remains that the London docks as we know them today were constructed
in the 19th Century when in the course of a few decades London became the
greatest and the most prosperous port in the world. The London Docks were the
busiest and at that time the best ever known to history. They were also the home
of the cockney London docker, famous for his strength, his language and his
capacity for porter.

He and his docker pals would have given little thought to the fact that the sacks
of lentils from India and the mutton from Australia they carried on their broad
shoulders would end up as soup and broth in thousands of working class homes
like their own.

In their heyday the London docks were one of the greatest sights of the world
– a hooting, clanging, whistling and shouting mass of men and machinery. I
remember myself as a young sailor going to sea for the first time in the early 50's
passing row after row of berthed ships loading and unloading their cargo as we
were tugged out of the Royal Albert Docks on our way to the Far East. All this
has now gone and no ships steam up the Thames to berth in London. Yuppies and
office workers have replaced the cockney dockers and the noise of the mighty
ships has been replaced by the whine of small airliners from the City Airport
ferrying business executives to Amsterdam, Brussels and Paris.

Mutton Broth

The proportions of the ingredients of this cheap and sustaining dish can be varied very widely without the final results being any less tasty. All you have to do is to buy as much of the cheaper cuts of mutton you can afford and ask your butcher to chop it up for you. Incidentally, he will not give you scrag end of mutton. He'll give you scrag end of lamb: these days all the lovely mature and strong flavoured mutton goes to the cat food factory – lucky pussy cats!

Put the meat into a saucepan with a few handfuls of pearl barley, a chopped carrot or turnip or preferably both, parsley, thyme and a little salt. Simmer for an hour and a half or until the meat comes away from the bones. Skim from time to time to remove any globules of fat.

With chicken so cheap these days, you can do an equally sustaining broth by substituting the cheapest of chicken you can buy for the scrag end.

Calf's Foot Broth

Very gently – and I mean very gently – stew a calf's foot in three pints of water, with a couple of strips of lemon peel. Stew until the liquid is reduced by half, removing any scum as it forms. Remove the calf foot and allow the liquid to cool. When it is quite cold take off every trace of fat. Warm up this broth and to every half pint, add a heaped teaspoon of sugar, a teaspoon of butter and a pinch of nutmeg. Take off the heat and add the yolk of one egg to every half pint and reheat stirring all the time until the mixture thickens. On no account allow the broth to boil after you have added the egg yolk or it will curdle. This was reputed to be very good for 'peaky' children.

Gruel

Gruel is a thin infusion of oats in water – a kind of super-diluted porridge. It is not very sustaining but it could just about keep body and soul together in a hard time. It will not surprise you that it was staple fare in workhouses.

If you have an upset stomach or are suffering from over-indulgence a short diet of gruel does you no harm at all. You simply boil a couple of handfuls of oatmeal in a pint of water, strain it – and there's your gruel. You can flavour it with a little salt or sugar or a grating of nutmeg.

Leftovers

In cockney households every penny
counted, so there was little waste.
Cockney housewives became very
ingenious at turning leftovers into
nourishing and tasty dishes. Some of
them were simple variations of more
elaborate recipes. Others combined
unusual ingredients or prepared
ordinary ingredients in unusual ways.
Some of them were so good they became
upwardly mobile and began to grace
middle-class or aristocratic tables.

Hopping

One of the traditional seasonal activities of cockney women and children was
'hopping' – gathering the ripe hops in the hopfields of Kent. This autumn holiday
lasted about a month and was eagerly looked forward to, both as an opportunity
to earn a little much-needed money but also a chance to escape from the mean
streets and crowded tenements of Hoxton and Poplar into the fresh air of the
countryside for a few magic weeks. For all-too-many cockney families it was
their only holiday – although it was never less than very hard and ill-paid work
for small children and their grannies as well as their mums.

The cockney hop-parties were picked up by horse and cart or, latterly, by open
lorry at the beginning of the harvest season and whole families would soon be on
their way with their bundles of clothes and their 'hopping pots' – the utensils with
which they cooked their stews and their strong, hot tea. Their accommodation
was the farm barns and sheds and the farmer would provide them with straw
mattresses and running water – and not much else. Everyone joined in pulling the
ripe hops from their vines and stuffing them into the huge sacks ready for the
journey to the familiar hop kilns. The big evening meal was prepared in the
knowledge that anything left over was for the next day's meal. Then the fires
were lit, and the games, songs and stories started, going on long into the night.

When all the hops were picked and the autumn nights drew in, the carts or
lorries would soon arrive to take them back to the East End – brown, healthy and
with money in their purse. Then the parlour of their favourite pubs would be
regaled with the familiar stories of the high old time they had.

impsons, the famous
estaurant in the
Strand, serves this dish
ɔ its customers.

Bubble and Squeak

Simply mashed up leftover potatoes combined with leftover cabbage. All together they are fried in hot dripping. The proportions do not matter as long as there is more potato than cabbage, or spinach or sprouts, or any other cooked green vegetables.

The great thing about bubble and squeak is that it should be well browned. It is the brown bits that give it its wonderful taste and I am not above mixing it about with the kitchen slice to expose more of the inside so that it gets browned too.

Shepherds' Pie

Again, a very simple but delicious dish. Basically, minced leftover meat topped with mashed potato and baked.

I must admit that I prefer to use lean minced beef, chopped onions, fresh thyme and parsley, salt and pepper, moistened with stock (a beef or chicken stock cube, dissolved in a little water will do), topped with creamy mashed potato. Bake this in a medium oven for an hour. The proportions don't matter, use what ever you have. It's an infinitely variable dish.

o not despise this
imple pudding. They
erve it in London's
amous Connaught
otel.

Bread and Butter Pudding

An excellent way of using up stale bread – and you can always let bread go stale, if necessary.

Thickly butter a pie dish and as many slices of stale, but not too stale bread. Line the dish with them, using plenty of currants, raisins and sultanas sprinkled over and between the slices of bread until the dish is filled with buttered bread and fruit. Beat two eggs into a pint of milk with two ounces of sugar. Pour this mixture over the bread and dredge the surface with more sugar. Leave to soak for an hour. Dredge with more sugar and bake in a moderate oven for thirty minutes.

Mince on Toast

Cockney butchers would mince up the odd bits of meat left at the weekend and sell the mince that was produced very cheaply. Cockney mothers would mix it with chopped onions, season it with pepper and salt, cook it with a little water and serve the savoury mixture on well-done toast. I still make this for myself quite often, intentionally burning the toast a little. The contrast between the burnt and crackly toast and the hot and tasty mince is very agreeable.

Rabbit Dishes

Until myxamatosis almost wiped them out, rabbits were very common all over Britain. Cockneys could buy them for a few pence. Cockney wives would know how to skin and gut them – selling the skins for a few pence herself – but these days the butcher will give you the rabbit ready prepared.

If you go to the supermarket you can even buy boneless rabbit from China. They air-freight it in alongside all the other delicacies that we get from the Far East these days. It is of excellent quality and useful for about all rabbit dishes – and with very little preparation.

London Pride

The Cockneys' very own flower. Botanically, it is known as a pink flowered Saxifrage, Saxifrage Umbrosa, also 'none-so-pretty' and, mysteriously, 'St Patrick's cabbage'. But to the true Cockney it was always 'London Pride' and he grew it whenever he could spare a little room from his rhubarb.

It is a tough little flower and it grows well in poor soil and in poor light. In Victorian cockney London, it had to grow in an atmosphere that would choke a carthorse, thick with the sulphurous smoke of a million fuming chimneys. The Cockneys grew it as a pot plant too and it graced the windowsill of many a cockney front room.

At the height of the blitz in 1941, Noel Coward wrote a famous song about London Pride. It began:

> *"London Pride has been handed down to us*
> *London Pride is a flower that's free"*

He was quite right. Because in the years following the Blitz, alongside the willow herb that sprang up on the bombed sites, the brave little red stem of London Pride could be seen shyly poking their way up through the piles of shattered bricks and tiles. Today, when cockney car owners concrete over their small front gardens as space for their car, they often leave a little patch of soil on which they grow one or two plants of London Pride.

Rabbit Pudding

This is a fine old East End dish, which is well worth reviving. Take a jointed rabbit and cut the flesh away from the bones. I prefer to do this after I have cooked the rabbit pieces for ten minutes; it's messy but easier and pleasanter. Make a stock by putting the bones in a pan. Add an onion, a carrot, a stick of celery, bayleaf and peppercorns and simmer for an hour – or more if you have the time. Chop the rabbit flesh into bite-size pieces, flour and fry until brown. Line a pudding basin with suet pastry put in the cooked rabbit and a sprinkle of herbs, fresh or dried. Now pour in the stock you have made from the bones, cap with suet pastry, cover with grease-proof paper and steam for four hours. Very tasty.

Rabbit Stew

A rabbit stew is very simple. Put the jointed rabbit in a saucepan, cover with water, season with pepper and salt, add sliced onions, a couple of sliced carrots and any other vegetables you have handy – a turnip, parsnip, or a stick of celery. Bring to the boil and simmer until the rabbit is tender. Serve with boiled potatoes.

I must admit I do it a little differently these days, because I prefer more rabbit than vegetables. So I restrict myself to onions, carrots, a stick of celery and add a bay leaf and a couple of stalks of parsley.

Rabbit Pie

Use the same ingredients as given for rabbit stew but put in a pie dish and cover with short crust pastry and bake for an hour, you have a splendid rabbit pie.

You can serve this dish with dumplings and mashed potatoes.

Baked Rabbit

This is an interesting way of cooking a whole rabbit. Pepper and salt it, lay it on a trivet in a baking tray and cover with a few slices of bacon. Cook in a hot oven for an hour, removing the bacon slices ten minutes before serving. A young rabbit will cook more quickly.

Afters

Cockney Kids liked sweet and spicy
puddings – so did their dads. This was
reflected in the sweets – the 'afters'
that cockney mums served their
families. Cockney mums would have
been very price-conscious and known
when gluts of fruit were likely to hit
the market. So when apples were at
give-away prices, apple pies and apple
dumplings would appear on the menu.
The same went for plums, cherries,
and all the other fruit that appeared
on her local market stalls.

The Tallyman

When it came to buying relatively expensive articles such as furniture, clothing
and household goods, many cockney families simply couldn't afford to pay for
them outright. This was where the tallyman came in. For the Cockney he
represented what nowadays we call 'hire purchase'. The tallyman would allow his
cockney customer to purchase the item he wanted for a down payment and then
pay the rest of the price in instalments – plus, of course, substantial interest. As is
common with human nature, once the Cockney had acquired and enjoyed his new
possession, the visit of the tallyman became a much-disliked and resented
occasion, and the cockney had numerous tricks and strategies to avoid due
payment. However, the tallyman had not undertaken his profitable but onerous
task without suitable 'on the job' training and he generally had two tricks to
match his cockney client's one. He would have a 'minder' to persuade the
backslider to pay up and persistent defaulters could be given a very hard time
indeed.

The name of the tallyman came from the way his predecessors plied their trade.
Mediaeval tallymen would record their debts and their repayment by making
notches on special pieces of wood called 'tallies' because the number of notches
had to 'tally' with the paid and the outstanding debt. The man with the bunch of
sticks was no more popular than his nineteenth century counterpart with his little
black book.

Did you know that it was the burning of ancient wooden tallies in the House of
Lords that started the fire that destroyed the Houses of Parliament in October
1834? The ancient tallyman succeeded where Guy Fawkes failed.

Apple Dumplings

There were two ways of preparing apple dumplings – baking or boiling. Purists say that you should use short crust pastry for the baked apples and suet crust for the boiled. (*See recipe below*). Please feel free to do so, but cockney housewives used suet crust for both – and so do I.

Peel and core biggish apples, eating or cooking, fill the holes with mincemeat or clove-flavoured sugar, or brown sugar, currants and cinnamon, or, indeed, any other sweet mixture you like.

Cut out rounds of pastry big enough to completely wrap the apples – experience will soon teach you that the correct size is bigger than you think! Wrap the apples in the pastry, pinching the pastry firmly at the top. For baked apples, put the pinched end down on an oiled baking sheet and bake for thirty minutes (400°F Mark 6) oven and serve. I usually brush a little egg yolk over the dumplings to make them shiny.

Spotted Dick

This cockney favourite is now out of fashion as it is anything but slimming. But for a hungry cockney family it was the perfect answer – "What won't fatten won't fill" as cockney mums used to say.

Make a suet pastry – two parts of self-raising flour to one part of finely shredded suet, mixed with enough water to make a soft dough. Roll out to an oblong, spread raisins all over the top, pressing them in so that they stay in the pastry, turn over and do the same to the other side. Roll it up into a thick cylinder, stick in a few more raisins for luck, wrap in greaseproof paper and steam for two hours.

Originally served with a thin golden syrup sauce. This suited the very sweet teeth of those days. Today's East End kids prefer it with custard.

Jam Roly Poly

This is exactly the same as Spotted Dick but uses jam rather than fruit. Make the suet pastry, roll it out and smear thickly with your favourite jam – but on one side only. Roll this up, cover with greaseproof paper and steam for two hours.

Not Everyone's Taste

The very rich are used to eating all kinds of food that the middle class finds a little off-putting. But the rich and the East Enders have one thing in common – they both have no inhibitions in finding and eating really tasty foods. Tripe is a good example: properly prepared it is food for the Gods, beautifully flavoured and textured. Eels too are among the most delicate and aristocratic of tastes.

It is the middle classes who show caution. Within a generation they have learnt to accept foreign delicacies like squid, scampi, curries and dried fish. Yet, the majority still refuses to try many regional, but entirely British dishes, like jellied eels and tripe. They are missing a lot.

Pie and Eel Shops

There were once many dozens of these all over the East End but they went into a sharp decline in the latter half of the twentieth century. Now they are having a revival. They serve meat pies with mashed potatoes but their real distinction was their hot stewed eels in liquor, a delicate green sauce with parsley. You could have this with the pie too. Properly prepared hot eels are quite delicious. A long time ago this was a cheap and nourishing dish for poor Cockneys. It remains nourishing, but it is, alas, no longer cheap.

After several decades of slow decline, eel and pie shops are now becoming popular again – although they will never be the cheap working class eating establishments they once were. But more and more people are beginning to realise that eels are a fine and distinguished fish and the traditional ways of cooking them as exemplified in pie and eel shops can hardly be bettered.

Tripe and Onions

Readers of the first edition have said the onions are not optional, they are essential. One said, "Eating tripe without onions is like eating a white kid glove".

The traditional Lancashire dish was appropriated by Cockneys lock, stock and barrel. But the Cockneys showed none of the fine discrimination between the various kinds of tripe displayed by his Northern cousins. He knew one dish and one dish only. And he loved it. My own version cannot be very far from those prepared by cockney housewives.

Peel and thinly slice two large onions. Cut a pound of tripe into pieces the size of postage stamps. Simmer the two together in a pint of milk until the tripe is tender – about an hour. Now melt an ounce of butter in another saucepan and add enough plain flour until it forms a glossy yellow paste – about an ounce. Add the tripe and onions and stir until liquid thickens. Flavour with salt, pepper and a dash of nutmeg. Serve in shallow bowls.

I myself always add a few small onions halfway through the cooking process because it makes the finished dish more attractive.

Jellied Eels

Take a large live eel, a sharp knife – perhaps you'd better let the fishmonger do this for you. Cover the chopped eel with water in a saucepan, add a bayleaf and a few peppercorns and boil gently until the eels are tender. Eels take between half an hour to an hour to cook through, depending on the size and thickness of the fish. It is done when a knitting needle or something similar pierces it to the bone easily. Cool and refrigerate.

This should produce a beautiful clear jelly with the chopped eel floating in it. Add pepper, salt and vinegar to taste. I find this a most delicate and refined dish – and the price of eels these days is beginning to reflect it.

An eel's skin contains most of the oil in the fish, so unless you are on a very strict diet, you should eat them skin and all. But if you really must skin an eel, and you cannot find a fish monger to do it for you, here is how to go about it. Cut off its head and run a sharp knife under the first half-inch of skin at the cut end of the fish (it will separate quite easily). Ease it back little by little all round when you will find it will peel back – just like taking off a glove.

Another first edition reader's note: if the fishmonger cuts the eel's head off, ask for it. It helps make the jelly.

Minus the Squeak

Old fashioned East End pork butchers
would tell their customers that they
could eat every part of the pig except its
squeak. Indeed they were right –
because there exist recipes for its liver
and lungs, its ears and tail, and, of
course, its intestines. The French have a
whole cuisine devoted exclusively to the
pig and its bits and pieces and the
French never go wrong where food is
concerned.

Although most butchers will not have
the interesting parts of the pig on
display, I have always found that they
are very willing to oblige if you ask for
anything unusual. Try your own
butcher and see.

Smithfield

London's great meat market, Smithfield is where 3,000 people today buy, sell,
prepare, carry and store the 350,000 tons of beef, lamb, pork and offal that passes
through its portals each year.

It is only comparatively recently that Smithfield has been a meat market pure
and simple. In Victorian times it was a vast abattoir as well, with blood and guts
everywhere and a stench that would knock you over. No place for a sensitive
stomach! Before that it had been a live cattle and horse market, and droves of
cattle, herds of sheep and other animals were a familiar – and unpopular – sight
on the streets of London. You can still find the granite troughs of the
Metropolitan Cattle Trough and Drinking Fountain Association in many parts of
London, thoughtfully placed there for the comfort of these animals.

Earlier still, Smithfield had a deservedly sinister reputation as a place of public
execution. Mary Tudor burned over two hundred martyrs here and a large number
of criminals were hanged, drawn and quartered, burned, beheaded, boiled and
roasted there to the edification and entertainment of Londoners.

Cockney butchers or street traders came here to buy their beef, mutton and
pork, or more especially, the cowheel, trotters, tripe and chitterlings that their
cockney customers loved so much.

The French make their famous 'andoulles' – sausages – from humble chitterlings.

Chitterlings

Chitterlings are the carefully cleaned and prepared small intestines of the pig – final proof that you can eat everything of a pig. Although they seem a bit odd to middle-class ears they are a delicate dish, much loved by both peasant and gourmet. As is so often the case, the people in the middle just don't know what they are missing.

Cockneys prepared them in a number of ways. I like them boiled and cold (they jelly easily) with salt, pepper and vinegar or rolled in seasoned flour and fried until they are crisp and brown on the outside but soft and tasty inside.

Plugger

This was popular with Cockneys because it could be made with the little scraps of bacon left after slicing on a machine – and they were very inexpensive. You needed the same weight of onion as bacon, chopped finely, seasoned with pepper (the bacon will supply all the salt necessary!) and moistened with a little water. Make some suet crust (*see recipe*), roll it out into a strip about a third of an inch thick, spread the bacon mixture over it and roll it up.

The Cockneys would have tied this up in a cloth but you will find greaseproof paper or foil easier. When it is well-sealed, boil it gently for about two hours. Excellent with pease pudding. I assume the name comes from the fact that it plugged a hungry feeling very successfully.

Pigs' Fry

This was a popular dish with cockney butchers who knew where to find the best meat and how to cook it. Pigs' fry were small pieces of a pig's interior – heart, liver, lungs and chitterlings – cut into slices, rolled in flour, seasoned with salt and pepper and fried in the pigs own fat. Serve piping hot with brown sauce.

Pigs' Ears

The butcher will have cleaned and singed these for you. Put a couple of them in a pan of water with salt, a sliced carrot, an onion, and a sprig or two of any herb you have, then simmer gently until tender – about an hour. You can cook pig's tail in the same way.

Most hungry Cockneys ate them right away with parsley or a sharp sauce but cooked trotters and tail can be grilled if you wish. Cut the trotters in half, lengthways, and brush them with lard or butter, roll in breadcrumbs and then grill very slowly. Pigs' tails can be treated in the same way.

All of these go well with boiled or mashed potatoes and haricot beans.

War Years

Wartime rationing during both World Wars was hard on women trying to feed their family. An additional hardship for all Londoners during the Second World War was the blitz, months of aerial bombardment.

However, nutrition experts now believe that the diet of those children treated during the latter war was far superior to that of many a present day-child. The shortages meant that children had a minimum of sugar and cholesterol and ensured a reasonably balanced diet.

The Blitz on the East End

For wartime German aircrews, bombing London was a doddle: you simply couldn't miss. For London's East Enders it was less fun – because they were the nearest part of London to the German air bases and the softest and easiest target on which the Dorniers and Heinkels could dump their bombs – the docks, the airfields, and the great munitions factories at Dagenham and Woolwich.

Only a few of the bombs found these targets. The vast majority of them fell on the narrow, crowded streets of the East End, causing enormous destruction among the small houses and tenements, killing and maiming thousands of their inhabitants. A big bomb could destroy a street and incendiary bombs could cause fires that quickly spread through the dry old timbers of the closely packed homes.

Bombed and blasted night after night after night through the dreadful winter of 1940-41, London's East Enders responded magnificently. When the 'all-clear' sounded, they would emerge from their basements and shelters to dig out their wounded and dead from the wreckage and clear up the broken glass from their own damaged homes. Bombed-out families would be found temporary shelter. The poor shared what little they had with the poorest of the poor. A strong community spirit of shared danger soon emerged and forged a fighting spirit that no German bombs could ever destroy.

Mock Banana

Imported fruit was rarely seen during the War. Children grew up without ever seeing a lemon, an orange or a banana.

As a substitute for bananas, parsnips were boiled until they were soft and mushy, mixed with as much sugar as could be spared and spread on bread for kids who had never tasted bananas. An early kind of 'junk food' and not without possibilities as the basis for a modern dish!

Mince Slice

This is an old recipe used in many working class homes. It has the advantage of using any left over cooked meat and takes very little time to cook. A version of this dish was recommended by the wartime Ministry of Food.

Mince any surplus cooked meat. For every two ounces of meat mix an ounce of mashed potatoes and an ounce of breadcrumbs. Season and add a pinch of herbs. Roll out on a floured board and shape into an oblong between a quarter and half an inch thick. Cut into slices and fry in hot fat for five minutes. To keep down the fat content, these slices can be grilled instead of fried.

Mint Tea

Rationing meant that even the cockney's cup of 'char' was in short supply. One way of making it go further was to use mint. The method was simple. Freshly made weak tea was poured into a jug with its bottom covered with sprigs of mint. The mint tea was strained and then served.

You can, of course, make it with boiling water rather than weak tea but few cockneys would have sacrificed the taste of tea, however weak. A belief in the therapeutic value of mint tea remains and you will still be offered mint tea in some older East End homes. But it is just as likely to be made from dried as from fresh mint and to my taste, less refreshing.

Sausage Slice

Another traditional recipe which was revamped by the Ministry of Food and called of all things 'Mock Duck'. Spread an inch layer of sausage meat in the bottom of a well-greased baking tin. Add an inch layer of minced apples sprinkled with dried sage. Top with a second layer of sausage meat. Cover with grease-paper and bake in a moderately hot oven for forty-five minutes.

"Taters'

Sadly, the days are long gone when the cockney housewife could tell her Majestics from her King Edwards and exactly which colour, size and shape of potato was proper for roasting, chipping, boiling and baking. Even more sadly, most greengrocers these days don't seem to know the difference – or care. However, supermarkets seem to do better at recommending the best use for potatoes on their shelves. I have found as a very rough guide that big potatoes with white flesh are best for boiling or baking and medium-sized yellow or waxy fleshed potatoes are best for chipping, frying or roasting.

The old wives story about the best part of the potato lying directly under the skin is absolutely true and it's more economical too, as any cockney housewife would have told you.

Pearly Kings and Queens

Costermongers were always 'flash' dressers fond of colourful scarves and extravagant ornament. At some point during the middle of the 19th Century, some of them got into the habit of sewing little lines of pearl buttons on the seams of their clothes. The most popular of them, their leaders and spokesmen, (and often, literally, fighters) against officious policemen and organised thugs, were encouraged to distinguish themselves by elaborating these decorations into patterns of pearl buttons.

Finally, in 1870, a famous costermonger called Henry Croft appeared in a suit totally covered in pearl buttons; the 'Pearly Kings' were born. He soon attracted many dozens of imitations, many of whom either by election or by sheer effrontery, staked out territory in London. Pearly Kings and Queens, in fact, appeared as far afield as Stevenage.

A pearly suit could weight as much as 60 pounds and today the buttons alone would be worth almost a thousand pounds. Henry Croft died in 1920 and his coffin was followed by four hundred 'pearlies'! In the spring of 1974 one of his suits was found in an old suitcase in a loft in Romford.

e very best mashed
otato comes from the
lesh of potatoes that
ave been baked
ather than boiled.

Jacket Potatoes

Still, to my mind, the best way of cooking a potato. You'll need a hot oven and well-scrubbed potatoes. Put them in the top of the oven and bake, one and half hours for medium-sized, two hours for whoppers.

Some people put a small cross-cut on top to prevent bursting and then put a knob of butter in this opened cross before serving. I myself prefer to leave the potatoes uncut and if they burst, treat this as a bonus, putting the butter (or whatever) where the potato has burst and perhaps slightly browned. It is a matter of taste.

For cockney mothers, one large baked potato for every family member was the ideal cheap meal. She would have served her hot potatoes with either a knob of butter, some grated cheese, fried onions, tomato sauce and any other cheap and tasty filling. I find that old potatoes are better than new for baking because their thicker skins crispen up more easily.

Hotpot

The Cockneys had their own version of this popular dish as, indeed, did every other part of the country. For it you'll need a big, deep oven-proof dish and a couple of pounds of neck of lamb or scrag or chump end, as the cockney housewife would have called it. Ask your butcher to chop it up for you.

Grease the inside of the pot. I always use butter wrappers, and line it with thick slices of potato. Put in the chopped meat along with two or three thinly sliced onions, half a dozen big sliced mushrooms, a couple of sliced carrots and a good seasoning of pepper and salt. Now cover the whole thing with a thick layer of sliced potatoes – or even two. Pour in a pint of water (stock is better, even if it is beef cube stock) and cover with a piece of buttered paper (the used butter wrapper is perfect for this).

Put in a moderate oven and cook for two hours. Now remove the paper, turn up the heat and cook until the top layer of potatoes is nicely browned – about half an hour. An excellent family dish. If you happen to have a butcher who can get you mutton instead of lamb, this dish is even tastier.

Cheese Pie

Layer mashed potatoes, grated cheese and onions in a buttered casserole, topping with grated cheese and sliced tomatoes. Bake in medium oven for twenty minutes then brown under a grill.

Shellfish

One of the few remaining relics of the cockney past are the shellfish stalls, often outside pubs, with their basins of whelks, cockles and jellied eels to be served on little plates with salt, pepper and vinegar. These days they can be found all over London and are likely to be selling shrimps, mussels, prawns and sometimes even oysters and Dublin Bay prawns. One of the most famous of these stalls was Tubby Isaacs at Aldgate but there are still many others.

Southend

During the summer months, every weekday evening, a little old train would wend its way across the North and East London, stopping at every small station to pick up passengers, often whole families. The train was known locally as the 'Cockle Special', and its destination was Southend.

Southend was the cockney's favourite seaside resort. It was near – twenty miles from London. It was cheap – there were always special cut-price tickets. And Southend had everything!

Southend had a pier – the longest in Britain (one mile). Southend had a music hall. Southend had a fairground for the kids. Southend had boat trips, donkey rides, peepshows. Southend had fish and chip shops, pie and eel shops and whelk stalls. Best of all, Southend had pubs. Lots of pubs.

The general idea was to put down a good layer of fish and chips, whelks and several plate of cockles (hence the name of the train). This would then be topped up by several pints of beer for Dad, a few glasses of stout for Mum, and a couple sarsaparillas for the kids who played outside. There would be the occasional wail from a kid getting his ear clipped for being cheeky, or for whining that he wanted to go home.

Then, when the light began to fade, the satisfied family would stroll to the railway station, conveniently close to the front, where the gently steaming 'Cockle Special' would be waiting to take them home to Ilford, Bethnal Green, or Holloway.

Cockles and Mussels

These can be bought in their shells alive or ready prepared. In this case they only need serving with pepper, salt and vinegar. Wash them thoroughly first to get rid of any lurking sand.

If you buy them in their shells from a fishmonger, wash them thoroughly and throw away any whose shells have opened – they are dead. Put the rest in a saucepan and heat over a fierce flame shaking the pan from time to time. They will soon open and release their juice. As soon as they have opened, remove from the heat.

Take the mussels and cockles out of their shells. Eat them with pepper, salt and vinegar. There are more complicated ways of preparing them but nothing a cockney would recognise.

Whelks

I have never cooked these and do not know anyone who has. They are prepared near to where they are gathered, on the East coast of Britain and I understand they are dropped into boiling water which is then immediately allowed to cool – boiling them makes them tough.

As it is, these gristly gastropods make a pretty chewy mouthful. But they taste of the sea and once you have acquired the taste, you'll find them irresistible. They are sold in fresh fish shops in their shells, which means you have to work them out with a pin. But at shellfish stalls, this has been done for you. The bigger they are, the tougher!

Winkles

A great favourite, bought like shrimps, from shop, stall or basket. They are sold ready cooked by the pint. If you have the opportunity to gather your own winkles from the rocks by the seashore, drop them into boiling water for twenty minutes, remove and let cool.

Eating technique is simple. Take a large plate of bread and butter alongside the bowl of winkles and provide each person with a small plate for the shells and the little brown cap, behind which the winkle hides itself, and a large pin. You take a slice of bread and butter and insert the pin into the whortled little shell and winkle out your winkle, discarding the empty shell and cap. Great fun.

Rhubarb

Rhubarb was introduced into Britain less than two hundred years ago, so we still have not had time to decide whether it is a fruit or a vegetable. But it is always treated as though it is a fruit in the various pies, fools and crumbles we cook today. It also produces an excellent home made wine. The cockney housewife would have known nothing of this and would have stuck firmly to the crumble 'afters' and jams with which she was familiar.

Free Fertiliser

In the 1850's the London Board of Health estimated that horses deposited more than 200,000 tons of manure on the streets of London every year. A fair proportion of this fell in the East End. Now Cockneys always had an eye on the main chance and very early on they realised that London horses were supplying them with a vast and continuous supply of free fertiliser. They also realised that the juicy stalks of rhubarb grew bigger and juicer when encouraged by the liberal application of this handy fertiliser. So wherever possible they planted crowns of rhubarb.

This plant had another advantage it will grow without too much light. This made it ideal for the sun-starved gardens and back yards of many East End streets. The cockney housewife would soon have worked out for herself that the juicy young stalks were best for rhubarb sweets like crumble and 'afters' and that the thick tough stalks were best reserved for making jam. For those who could find a really sunny spot there was also the chance to grow a few marrows on the manure heap. Unlike other parts of the country there is little evidence that Cockneys grew marrows competitively, with each trying to grow one larger than his neighbour. In the East End they were grown strictly for food and were all the better for it.

Rhubarb Crumble

For every pound of rhubarb you need two tablespoons of golden
syrup, one and a half ounces of margarine, four ounces of plain
flour and three ounces of sugar. Cut the rhubarb into small
pieces. Simmer it with the syrup until soft and put it into an
ovenproof dish. Rub the margarine into the flour with a pinch of
salt and the sugar until it has the texture of breadcrumbs.
Sprinkle over the stewed fruit. Bake in a moderate oven for
fifteen minutes.

Rhubarb Jam

You will need for every pound of rhubarb a pound of sugar and
the rind of half a lemon. Try to use young rhubarb but if it is
stringy, peel it, put the sugar, grated lemon and rhubarb in a pan
and gently heat until the sugar is dissolved, stirring all the time.
Then turn up the heat and as soon as the jam begins to boil,
turn down and simmer until the jam sets, skimming off any
scum that comes to the surface. How long setting will take
depends very much on the rhubarb. If it is young, three-quarters
of an hour will be sufficient, but old rhubarb may need one and
a half hours.
 Pour into warmed pots while hot, and seal.

Rhubarb Afters

In cockney terms this was a luxury dish requiring more
preparation than most 'afters'. For every pound of rhubarb you
need five ounces of sugar and two eggs. Use a large pan and
simmer the rhubarb in a couple of tablespoons of water with the
sugar until you get a thick smooth pulp. Then add the beaten egg
yolks, pour into an ovenproof dish and cook for thirty minutes in
a moderate oven.
 Suburban housewives still make a similar dish, fruit amber,
using any other fruit. If she tries rhubarb, as an economy, the
sweet is generally spoiled by using too much water and too small
a pan. The shrewd cockney housewife knew better.

Home Grown

Apart from the marrow on the manure heap, there were a number of vegetables and fruits the cockney gardener liked to grow. Runner beans on their rows of sticks were very popular, as were onions, tomatoes, peas and carrots. Few of them grew potatoes as these were very cheap to buy anyway.

Although they were never competitive gardeners like their fellow countrymen in the North of England, they often had little dodges and secrets which they kept jealously to themselves concerning how to grow the biggest and best produce.

Keeping an Allotment

The first allotments were allotted to people to grow their vegetables on as early as 1819 and by 1886 there were 650,000 allotments in Britain. Cockneys, ever fast to get on to a good thing, had more than their fair share of them and although there was little or no room in the tenemented and crowded streets of London, there were very large areas of unused land a few miles away at Tottenham, Walthamstow and Hackney marshes to the north and Greenwich and Erith marshes to the south.

These were a fair distance from the heart of the East End in anybody's book, but the Cockneys loaded their spades and forks and – always – a bucket for horse manure on their donkey shay or handcart and set off for their allotment whenever they had the time.

This land was not good but a few buckets of manure would work wonders. And on his own, private little patch of land the Cockney would grow his fancy.

During the War years, everyone was encouraged to have their own allotment. The authorities even dug up parks and commons to provide them.

Today the allotments are there in even greater numbers as London's land-starved citizens seek out a few square yards to grow their fruit flowers and vegetables. But today the rhubarb and marrows are likely to grow alongside all kinds of exotic produce and the Cockney to rub friendly shoulders with surgeons, architects and even, on my local allotment, a Peer of the Realm.

o one knows what
unkard dreamed up
is extraordinary
cipe but Cockneys
rtainly used it.

Marrow Rum

A chancy recipe in my view since it is a race between the
marrow disintegrating into a horrible mush and the collection of
the 'rum'.

Take a large, very ripe marrow, demerara sugar, an orange
and yeast. Saw off the stalk of the marrow and scoop out the
seeds with a large spoon. Fill the hole with sugar. Cream the
yeast with a little water and pour over the sugar. Squeeze the
orange and add the juice. Seal the top (I always use the stalk
plus sticky tape). Stand the marrow, base end down, on or in a
large jug or container. After a month or so you'll smell
fermentation, now make a small hole in the base with a knitting
needle so that the liquid inside can drain out. Collect and put in
a large jar with a fermentation lock as it will continue to
ferment. When it has finished fermenting, bottle it. Drink it.
Good luck!

Peas

resh young peas were a great favourite and a row of bright
reen pea plants was a common sight on cockney allotments.
lthough tinned peas were cheap, they never tasted as good as
e genuine article.

Young peas like this need only a few minutes in lightly salted
oiling water before they are succulently ready to serve. I always
dd a tiny spoonful of sugar. A sprig of fresh mint cooked with
e peas makes an enormous difference.

Preserved Beans

Like so many other things in life, the cockney gardener would
find that he would suddenly have too much of a good thing. All
his summer beans would ripen together and he would have
more than he knew what to do with.

His wife would take a large crock and cover the bottom with
a layer of salt. Then a layer of beans, topped, tailed and with
the stringy outside edges removed. Then more salt, more beans
and so on until the crock was full. A final thick layer of salt.
After a week or so the beans would have settled and a couple
more layers, salted as before, could be added.

To use the beans she would wash them thoroughly under cold
running water and cook them any way she preferred.

Soups

The Cockneys were not great soup drinkers but there were one or two soups that most cockney mothers would give their families when they were really hard up and could only afford the very cheapest ingredients. This would lead her away from meat and towards vegetables and dried pulses like lentils; dried peas and dried beans. On some recorded occasions cockney mothers took their families to market to glean vegetables that had fallen off the stalls. The word 'soup' to cockneys often reminded them of 'soup kitchens' and charity, so they were always regarded as second best to 'real' food.

The Watercress Girl

Henry Mayhew, in his famous 'London Labour and the London Poor' published in 1850, spent years exploring the slums of Victorian London. He tells of an eight year old girl who made her living from selling watercress.

'I asked her about her toys and her games with her companions: but the look of amazement that answered me soon put an end to any attempt at fun on my part. I then talked about the parks and whether she ever went to them. 'The parks!' she exclaimed in wonder 'Where are they?' I explained to her, telling her that they were large open places with green grass and tall trees where beautiful carriages drove about and people walked for pleasure and children played. Her eyes brightened up a little as I spoke and she asked half-doubtingly 'Would they let such as me go there, just to look?' All her knowledge seemed to begin and end with watercresses and what they fetched. She knew no more of London than the part she had seen on her rounds and believed that no quarter of the town was handsomer or pleasanter that it was at Farringdon market or at Clerkenwell where she lived.'

Celery Soup

You will need one head of celery, an ounce of ground rice, two pints of water or meat boilings (stock), half a pint of milk, seasoning, two yolks of egg and two ounces of butter.

Use all the white and tender green part of the celery, and wash and shred it finely. Throw it into a saucepan of boiling salted water, scald for ten minutes, then strain and rinse again in cold water.

Melt half the butter in a soup pot, put in the celery and cook it slowly for about fifteen minutes. Mix the ground rice smoothly with water or meat stock and then simmer slowly until the celery is tender – about one hour.

Rub as much as possible through a sieve, rinse out the pot and return the puree to reheat. Beat up the yolks of egg with the milk, strain into the soup, stir until thoroughly hot, but do not boil again. Add the remainder of the butter just before serving. Serve with hot crusty bread.

Watercress Soup

This is basically potato soup flavoured with watercress. So in the season when watercress was very cheap it was an economical and nourishing family meal.

Boil, drain and mash a pound of potatoes, mix in a pint and a half of milk, and a teaspoon of salt, reheat for ten minutes before serving, put in the chopped leaves of a bunch of watercress. I myself put in a large knob of butter and a good grind of black pepper but cockney households would not have been so extravagant. The watercress stalks, I boil alongside the potatoes for extra flavour, taking them out before mashing.

You can use a liquidiser instead of a sieve but you will lose the authentic texture.

Pea Soup

This is another simple classic, consisting of split peas, soaked overnight, simmered in salted water until they have softened. Again the state of your purse dictated the thinness or thickness of the soup.

For modern tastes, soak half a pound of split peas overnight. Put the soaked peas in water and bring to the boil. Strain this first water off and add two pints of hot water. Add a sliced onion and carrot, a big knob of butter and a teaspoon of sugar. Bring to the boil and simmer until tender. This will take anything between two and three hours.

When the peas are tender and mash easily, put them through a coarse sieve, add pepper and salt to taste and reheat.

Corned Beef

A disparaging description of a cockney housewife was that "she cooked with a tin opener". But canned food has brought a wide range of cheap meals to households once dependent on local produce. In 1810 an Englishman, Peter Durand took out a patent to preserve food in tin-coated iron cans; ten years latter he was supplying canned food to the Royal Navy. Soon the process was taken up in the USA, already producing massive food surpluses. 'We eat what we can and can what we can't' was the motto from which Europe benefited. Canning introduced the East Enders to corned beef and they soon found plenty of interesting ways to use this convenience food. Alas, no British company cans corned beef any more. Today's tins are all imported.

The Match Girls

The Cockneys have always felt they are a close community with a duty to help each other. This was demonstrated when in 1888 the match girls at Bryant & Mays factory came out on strike. It was the first time in Britain that unorganised women workers had taken such action. Most East Enders knew little about 'working class solidarity' and not much about trade unionism but the strikers found their fellow Cockneys right behind them.

There was no doubt that the match girls had a just case. Always at risk from 'flossy jaw' an industrial disease caused by the phosphorus they handled, adult women earned no more than nine shillings a week (45p); juniors were paid half that amount.

Boosted by local support, it was not long before sympathy spread beyond the East End. Help was given by social reformers like Sydney Webb and the playwright Bernard Shaw. Newspapers took up the match girls cause. After a fortnight Bryant & Mays gave in. Arbitration secured higher wages and the end of a system allowing fines to be deducted from the woman's wages.

Corned Beef Pie

Prepare or buy 12 ounces of short crust pastry, roll out and use half to line a pie dish. Fry one chopped onion in ½ an ounce of butter or a tablespoon of oil until transparent. Mash the onion with 12 ounces of corned beef (2 cans), add 8 ounces of mixed cooked diced vegetables, such as carrots, peas, green beans and mushrooms, then put in an egg and a teaspoon of Tabasco sauce, season and mix well. Place on top of the pastry in the dish and use the remaining pastry as a covering. Cook in a preheated moderate oven for 30 minutes. This dish can be served cold.

Corned Beef Hash

Mix 12 ounces of diced cooked potatoes, a large chopped onion, 2 ounces of corned beef, a ¼ pint of beef stock season and add teaspoon of Worcester sauce. Melt one ounce of butter and spread the mix in the pan. Cook slowly after about 40 minutes. A thick delicious crust will form on the bottom. It is now ready to eat.

Corned Beef Mould

Mix together 6 ounces of corned beef, 6 ounces of soaked bread, 6 oz mashed cooked carrot, 2 tablespoons of horse radish, chopped parsley, 2 teaspoons of mustard powder, and season. Press into a basin with a weight on top. Turn out, cut into slices. This goes well with a bulky salad and a good dollop of salad cream but the Cockneys were more likely to use these slices on buttered toast or as part of a packed lunch.

Cabbage and Corned Beef

Cockneys were not great lovers of greens but they were often cheap and, moreover, they knew that 'greens are good for you'. Heat ½ ounce of butter in a saucepan, add one sliced leek and fry. When soft, add one pound of corned beef cut into small cubes, a pound of diced cooked potatoes and sprinkle with the flour. Add ¼ pint of beef stock and ½ teaspoon of mustard. Heat until very hot, occasionally stirring. Meanwhile, cook a shredded cabbage by plunging it into salted boiling water, reduce the heat and cover. Cook for no more than 8 minutes. Drain, glaze with butter and serve immediately, topped with the corned beef mixture.

Eggs

While many people regard battery farming as barbaric, until its introduction chickens were expensive and rarely seen on East End tables. Eggs were different, cheap and nutritious. The favourite was fried eggs often turned over and cooked on both sides. Cooked on one side only it was 'sunny side up'. Two on a plate – the cockney male expected to be served this number – were 'two eyed steaks.'

Boiled eggs were popular. No one thought it childish to dip 'fingers' of buttered bread into their egg. Alas, like our chicken pieces, most eggs too are now the product of battery farming, and their taste has suffered.

Jack the Ripper

A popular East End trip for tourists is to visit the scenes of the crimes committed by Jack the Ripper. Between August to November 1888 seven prostitutes were murdered and horribly mutilated by knife.

The interest in these murderers has persisted for over a century, not so much from morbid interest but because the Riper was never caught. The brewers, Truman, named one of their East End Pubs Jack the Ripper.

Countless books have been written speculating on his identity though not even the killer's sex has been proved. Suggestions have ranged from his being a demented member of the Queen Victoria's family to one of a list of mentally sick lawyers, merchants and surgeons. A mad medic is the most popular choice. The bodies were dismembered in a way that only someone with a knowledge of surgery could have achieved.

In July 1889 there was a further victim found with her knifed torso spread over an alley not far from where the first murder had taken place. Was this a 'copy cat crime' or had the Ripper, after under four months of frenzied slaughter, waited a full year before claiming his final victim?

Omelettes?

There do not seem to be any records of omelettes being part of the Cockney's traditional diet but they certainly whipped eggs to which they added a little milk and fried these along with any suitable ingredients that were on hand. They called them egg fries. Sounds very much like an omelette! They tended to be rather solid and bulky but tasty just the same.

Here is a recipe for ham and potato fry. You can vary the ingredients, providing the eggs are at least a third of the volume of the other food in the pan. Fry a chopped onion and ½ a pound of diced potatoes in 3 ounces of butter until the potatoes are tender, then add 4 ounces of cooked chopped ham. Blend 5 eggs with 5 tablespoons of milk, pour over the mixture and cook for 6 minutes or until the eggs are set.

Scrambled Egg Mix

Whisk 8 eggs in a basin add 4 tablespoons of milk and season. Melt 4 ounces of butter in a saucepan and pour in eggs. Cook gently, stirring until the mixture starts to thicken. Remove from heat but continue stirring until creamy.

What about the mix? Scrabbled eggs are another food the Cockneys loved because you can give it zest and nourishment by adding anything suitable in the larder. Here are a few suggestions. 8 ounces of either cooked diced bacon, cooked diced ham or grated cheese. Or for a real luxury a small tin of crabmeat pieces.

Egg Ham Rolls

Scramble the eggs, as above, but use half the quantity and allow to cool. Chop 4 large skinned tomatoes and add these to the scrambled egg. Wrap the mixture in 8 slices of cooked ham. Tie with thin string if you wish. Put the rolls into a greased dish sprinkle with 5 ounces of cheese and cook in a moderate oven until the cheese starts to brown.

The Inner Man

Aggressive advertising by firms promoting proprietary laxatives convinced cockney housewives of the need for a weekly purgative for their children. A regular intake of one (disguised as a chocolate) was a common Friday night dose for many children.

However, long before the medical advocacy of high fibre diets, many enlightened cockney mothers were also convinced of the natural therapeutic value of prunes. So stewed prunes became a standard pudding.

Street Amusements

Although Cockneys were poor, they could always spare a penny for someone who made them laugh, astonished them or played upon their heartstrings. So there was a continuous street theatre in London's East End. First there was the familiar hurdy-gurdy man, endlessly turning the handle of his barrel organ with its twangling version of popular songs, usually with a little monkey rattling its tin for coppers. Then there was the spoons player whose only instrument was a couple of household spoons with which to rattle out his tunes. There was the bemuscled escapologist, challenging his onlookers to chain him up and then, easily escaping, passing the hat round among his amazed onlookers. There was also another musician whose act it was to produce sweet music by rubbing his finger round the rims of moistened glass tumblers.

Buskers played their various acts outside the pubs – always a good place for a generous collection. For the kids there was the man with his tiny hand-turned roundabout, easily set up on any street corner. Here too, and most popular of all, the Punch and Judy man would set up his booth and delight the children with the murderous fun of Mr Punch, Judy, the policeman and the crocodile. Few adults could resist this age-old show either. And at the sharp end there was the thimble-rig, where cockneys paid out good money being fooled, by not finding the pea under the thimble where they were so sure it had to be. 'Find the lady' was a popular con too: this famous three-card trick is still parting Londoners from their money – when the policeman isn't looking.

Stewed Prunes

Prunes are an excellent mild laxative and cockney mums would regularly serve them to their children as a sweet (with custard). All they did was to soak the prunes overnight and cook them the next day until they were plump and tender.

This simple method is very appetising but I prefer the treatment recommended by a modern successful cockney businessman. He assures me that his recipe is a popular treatment of a traditional food served in many smart modern cockney homes. Stew a pound of giant-sized prunes in a bottle of dry white wine with three ounces of sugar, a strip of lemon peel and a pinch of nutmeg. Beautiful!

Prune Roly

For every four ounces of cooked prunes, blend eight ounces of flour, two teaspoons of baking powder and a pinch of salt. Mix with milk until you get a soft dough. Roll out on a pastry board. Mix the prunes with two ounces of breadcrumbs, a tablespoon of golden syrup, three tablespoons of sugar and a teaspoon of spice. Spread this mixture over the pastry and roll, sealing in the prune mixture. Brush with melted margarine and put in the oven. Bake for one hour at a moderate heat.

Prunes with no refinements are now offered as part of the executive breakfast in many four-star hotels.

Devilled Prunes

The ingenious cockneys hit on an inexpensive version of the aristocratic 'Angels on horseback' a favourite delicacy in Ascot racegoers' lunch baskets. This was a cooked oyster wrapped in fried bacon and served cold. The Cockney simply wrapped a cooked stoned prune and treated it in exactly the same way, renaming it 'Devils on horseback'. This is quite a common and very tasty cocktail snack. The prunes should still be quite firm for this East End recipe.

Fry-Ups

Although Cockneys had not the facilities for proper deep frying, they liked fried, fatty foods, and the frying pan was one of the cockney housewife's favourite kitchen utensils. She used it for dishes as varied as fish cakes, bubble and squeak and the occasional chop or steak. Sensibly, she would never wash it but merely wipe it dry with a sheet of newspaper.

Today's housewife would probably use sheets of kitchen roll paper but the principle remains the same. The only thing to remember is to avoid using the pan for frying strong-flavoured fish like kippers. However hard you clean and scour, the kipper will announce itself for some fry-ups later!

The First Take-away

The national dish of Britain is traditionally 'the roast beef of old England' but if you look around you will not see many roast beef shops. On the other hand it is difficult, in any sizeable town, to be more than half a mile from a fish and chip shop. Although London has been famous for its cooked meat shops since the Middle Ages, fish and chip shops didn't make an appearance until the end of the nineteenth century. They were the first real 'take-aways' and very popular in London's East End which still boasts of having some of the best 'chippers' in Britain.

In fact, there are so many fish and chip shops, and the ways of preparing fish and chips so institutionalised, that it is hardly worth the trouble to cook fish and chips at home. There is an extra flavour to fish and chips from a proper 'chipper' that comes from the newspaper they were always wrapped and served in. This is, unfortunately, a rarity nowadays.

The success of the particular combination of fish dipped in batter and chopped potatoes depended on the technique both of keeping large amounts of fat very hot continuously and safely and the formulations of fat that would stand up to continuous very high temperatures.

Legend has it that the Italians discovered the secret in the preparation of their famous 'Fitto Misto Mare'. Whatever the answer, it certainly worked!

Fish and Chips

Make a batter by beating together four ounces of flour, a quarter of a pint of milk and two beaten eggs, all blended together and left to stand for an hour.

Heat cooking oil in a deep fryer until it is very hot. You can test this by throwing in a small piece of bread. If the fat bubbles around the bread, it is hot enough.

Dip pieces of the fish you have – cod, haddock, skate, rock salmon (dogfish) or whatever – into the batter and gently lower into the fat. Cook until the batter is crisp and brown.

For the chips, peel potatoes and cut lengthways into batons, lower these in a chip basket into another deep fryer full of very hot fat and fry until golden brown.

Fish Cakes

In some smart restaurants they serve exactly the same dish but always using tinned pink salmon in the fish ingredient. Very good too.

Another cheap potato dish was fishcakes. For this you need a lot of mashed potato, a variable quantity of fish, and a hot frying pan. The fish could be almost anything, usually cooked and often the cheapest tinned fish that could be bought. Tinned red salmon was particularly favoured. But, of course, the state of your pocket would determine both the quality and quantity of fish in the fish cake.

All you do is mash the fish well with the mashed potato, form into little flat cakes, fry and serve piping hot. Tomato sauce was and is the classical accompaniment to this dish.

Scallops

Dismiss from your mind any thoughts of succulent shellfish. These dietary horrors are cockney belly timber and nothing more.

Briefly, they are only mashed potato cakes dipped in batter and fried, preferably deep fried. The resulting depth-charge was served with strong brown sauce, the ingredients of which it was probably best not to know. Today use one of the highly respectable brown sauces, which you can find on the shelves of any grocer or supermarket.

Whatever their failings as a waistline reducer, I must admit that a hot crisp cockney scallop on a plate when you've just come in from a cold wet winter night has its attractions.

Cockney Drinks

The Cockney's preference for a strong
drink and over-boiled tea had a strong
common-sense basis. Until well into the
second half of the nineteenth century,
East End water was a highly dangerous
drink. In 1848-9, water-borne cholera
killed 14,000 Londoners and in 1866
5,000 died of the same disease in three
weeks.

Dr John Snow, Queen Victoria's
obstetrician, found the answer. He
persuaded the local authorities to
remove the handle from the public
water pump in the worst affected area.
The disease almost immediately
disappeared.

Great Boozers

If you wander through the East End of London on many street corners you will
see, standing out from their poor little neighbours, substantial buildings with lots
of elaborately carved stonework, expensive woodwork and big windows of etched
glass. Today these fine buildings are often banks, shops and offices.

Once they were pubs – hundreds and hundreds of them. There were few
cockney streets that didn't boast its own palatial pub because, although Cockneys
were very particular about where they ate, they were even more particular where
they drank – and drank – and drank.

Cockneys, it must be said, were great boozers. At the richer end they drank
London gin, with water or bitters or both, or brandy. The wives of these superior
cockneys usually drank port and lemon (port and lemonade). This truly awful
drink is only improved by the thought that the so-called port was likely to be even
worse if undiluted by the lemonade.

The broad mass of Cockneys drank Porter – something approaching latter day
mild or Burton. It was a sweet malty drink and they drank it by the barrelful.
Brewers grew rich on this beverage. Many of the most exalted members of the
aristocracy owe their titles to the sore heads of Cockneys.

Whatever the Cockneys drank, it had to be tasty and strong. This went for their
non-alcoholic drinks too. But it was the river of beer flowing through the many
hundreds of pubs that the Cockneys really floated on.

Porter

Porter was a dark brown, sweet malt liquor much loved by the cockney porters after which it was named. It was brewed not only by the large London breweries but by many dozens of the small family brewers.

Porter gradually faded out and was replaced by either mild or Burton or, latterly, the black and creamy stouts, especially Mackesons and, of course, Guinness.

London Gin

London gin has been around a long time and one of Hogarth's most famous paintings – 'Gin Lane', painted in the middle of the 18th Century, clearly shows that Londoners were familiar with it then. Bone dry London gin was supposed to be superior to Plymouth gin, which was sweeter. London gin was distilled – and very profitably – all over London in distilleries whose products varied from the dubious to the poisonous. You will be pleased to hear that the Gordons, Booths and Gilbeys of today are infinitely superior to the gin our forefathers drank.

Thankfully, it would be almost impossible to make a gin drink anything like those the cockneys downed. A pink gin, with Angostura and water, would probably come closest.

Tea

Cockneys liked their tea hot, strong and sweet. The brew they made had little in common with the Harrods-packed Darjeeling and Ceylon of Knightsbridge and Mayfair. It was bought in penny packets from a box at the grocer, anonymous, powdery and very, very cheap. Almost certainly most of it came from the sweepings of the great tea warehouses in the docks, most of which burned down in the blitz of 1941.

A spoonful of this 'tea' for every drinker – plus one for the pot – was the formula. The resultant dark brown liquid would be served in mugs and very often sweetened with condensed milk. Fresh milk was a doubtful commodity in cockney London. It must be said that the cloying sweetness of the condensed milk probably did take the sharp and bitter edge off the dark, strong tea but it would not be a taste much appreciated by the delicate palates of today.

RECIPE INDEX

GENERAL INDEX

Weights and Measures

The shrewd cockney housewife stocked up with whatever food was available at the lowest possible price or better still, free. She then decided how to use it. If possible, turning any surplus into pickles or preserves. In keeping with this tradition, whenever practical, proportions rather than suggested quantities are given.

Where this could be confusing, Imperial measurements are printed. A metric conversion table is given below, although the continental system would be quite unknown to Cockneys of the past – or the present for that matter.

Imperial Weights	Metric/Weights
The smallest weight given is an ounce	1 ounce = 28 grams
16 oz = 1 pound	4 ounces = 113 grams
14 lb = 1 stone	8 ounces = 226 grams
	1 pound = 453 grams

Metric/Imperial
30 grams = 1 ounce (approx)
100 grams = 3.5 ounces (approx)
250 grams = 9.0 ounces (approx)
1 kilogram = 2.2 pounds (approx)

Solid Measure

Butter or other fats	1 ounce 2 level tablespoons*	1 pound 2 cups
Flour	1 ounce 2 tablespoons	1 pound 4 cups
Castor sugar	1 ounce 1 level tablespoon	1 pound 2 cups
Icing sugar		1 pound 3 cups
Brown sugar		1 pound 2½ cups
Rice		1 pound 2 cups
Dried Fruit		1 pound 2 cups
Minced meat		1 pound 2 cups
Lentils and split peas		1 pound 2 cups
Fresh breadcrumbs		1 pound 4 cups
Water	1 pint	2½ cups

*Standard measuring tablespoon

Grill = USA broil